TEN BOYS WHO
DIDN'T GIVE IN

TEN BOYS WHO DIDN'T GIVE IN

LIGHT KEEPERS

Irene Howat

CF4·K

For John, Samuel and Joseph

Copyright © 2004 Christian Focus Publications
Reprinted 2005, 2006, 2007, 2009, 2011, 2013, 2015,
twice in 2017 and 2019
Paperback ISBN: 978-1-84550-035-1
epub ISBN: 978-1-84550-840-1
mobi ISBN: 978-1-84550-841-8

Published by Christian Focus Publications,
Geanies House, Fearn, Tain, Ross-shire,
IV20 1TW, Scotland, Great Britain.
www.christianfocus.com; email:info@christianfocus.com
Cover design by Alister MacInnes
Cover illustration by Elena Temporin,
Milan Illustrations Agency
Printed and bound in Turkey

All incidents retold in these stories are based on true situations. Where specific information about childhood incidents has been unobtainable the author has written these paragraphs using other information concerning family life, hobbies, home life, relationships freely available in other biographies.

The front cover depicts Nate Saint as a young boy, in 1928, fishing with his dog. It would be two years later before he took his first flight in an aeroplane, but he would eventually work as a pilot for Mission Aviation Fellowship. Nate Saint became one of the Auca Five - Missionaries who were murdered by the very tribes people they had tried to help.

Contents

Polycarp

The child had never felt so frightened in all of his life. And it wasn't helped one little bit that his mother was crying so hard, that it looked as though she would never stop.

'I don't want to go away and leave you,' said Polycarp. 'I want to stay here at home with you for ever.'

His mother tried to pull herself together. Wrapping her son in her arms, she whispered into his ear.

'I wish you could stay here with me too, my son. But slaves don't make decisions; they are told what to do. And we've been told that the time has now come for you to be sold to another master. It may be that he will be a kind man and not work you too hard.'

Recognising the effort his mother was making, young Polycarp did the same. He wiped the tears from his cheeks, undid himself from his mother's arms, and stood as tall and straight as he could.

'I'll work hard,' he said. 'And even if my new master is not a kind man, I'll work so hard that he'll come to respect me. When I'm grown up, he'll maybe put me in charge of all his slaves, and I promise I'll be good to them if he does.'

Smiling through her tears, the woman nodded.

'I know you will, my son. I know you will.'

For the last time, she sat by his mat in the darkness of their poor home and told the boy a story before he went to sleep.

'This is the story of a slave family,' she began, 'a family just like our own. They had a son about your age whom their master didn't want to keep. So, he was taken to the slave market where he stood with all the other child slaves waiting to be bought by new masters. Strange men came and looked at them, felt their arm and leg muscles and looked to see if their eyes were clear and if they were free from obvious diseases. Eventually, a man approached the boy. He looked him up and down, turned him round, asked his age and what he was good at. Then the man walked away. The boy was just beginning to breathe normally again when the man reappeared with the market official.

"I'll take that one," the man said.

The official cut the rope that bound the boy to his neighbours on either side, though he left his hands tied together. Not knowing what lay before him, and whether he would ever see his parents again, the boy slave went with his new master into his new life, determined to make the very best of it.'

Polycarp knew his mother was preparing him for what was to come.

'Did the boy ever see his parents again?' he asked quietly.

His mother smiled sadly. 'I don't know the end of the story, my son,' she said. 'I only know that when the boy went to his new master, he went bravely.'

Kissing him goodnight for the very last time, the woman wrapped herself in her sadness and curled up tight on her mat on the floor.

Polycarp had no sleep at all that night, not a single wink. 'Is that how I'll be sold?' he wondered. Then a shudder ran right through his thin body. 'Will I be tied up in the slave market, or has the master already arranged where I'll be going? Will I ever see Dad and Mum again?' The whole night was full of questions and shudders that seemed to shake his whole world, then more and yet more questions. In the first light of dawn, he looked across the room at his mother, and his heart gave such a lurch he thought he was going to be sick. Then, just as he thought he could be no more miserable, his mother stirred. It was time she was up and at work. Pretending to be asleep, Polycarp put a hand over his eyes so that he could watch what she was doing between his fingers. Before she left to begin her day's work, the poor soul knelt beside her son, laid her hand on his shoulder, and whispered near his ear, 'Be brave, my son. And I will be brave for you.'

Later that morning, Polycarp discovered that he had a mistress rather than a master, a mistress named Calisto. New things seemed to come at him from all sides, so much so that by evening he felt as though he'd got up in a rush in the morning and put his head on backwards! And when bedtime came, it seemed like he'd closed the door of one world and opened the door of another, and somehow it didn't seem quite as scary as he thought it would be. The boy hoped his mother knew where he was and what kind of home he'd gone into.

'She won't worry so much if she knows,' thought Polycarp.

And that was certainly true, though we don't know whether his family knew or not.

The years that followed were very different from the ones that had gone before. As a little boy, when Polycarp's master clapped his hands, everyone jumped to attention and did exactly what they were ordered. Nobody ever asked a slave to do things; they gave orders that had to be obeyed. He had had enough food, but only just. And the cloth of his tunic was the cheapest in town, and it was covered in darns and patches. His bed had been a mat on the floor, and the nearest he ever got to a book was when he had to carry one to his master. As he settled down in Calisto's home, the boy thought back to his 'old days'.

One night, he lay in bed thinking over all the changes that had come about in his life.

'There's the bed to start with,' Polycarp smiled. 'I don't sleep on the floor now because I've got my own straw mattress. There are no patches on my tunics. Then he grinned. It was tunics, not tunic. He had three, one to wear and two to change with. No wonder they didn't wear through and need patching! 'And what would Mum say if she knew I was learning to read and write?' The truth of it was that Calisto was bringing Polycarp up as her son, not as a slave in her household. Eventually the day

11

came when the boy realised that servants were looking after his needs rather than him being a servant. He remembered his promise to his mother and was good to them.

We don't know how it happened, but we do know that by the time Polycarp was a man he had come to faith in the Lord Jesus Christ. That was the biggest blessing in his life, but there was another blessing too. When Calisto died, she left Polycarp everything she owned! The little slave boy had become a wealthy and educated man in the ancient town of Smyrna. (Smyrna is now known as Izmir, and it is on the west coast of Turkey.)

Polycarp's money didn't make him self-centred; instead he used it to help spread the good news about Jesus Christ.

'Sometimes I wish I'd been born a hundred years ago,' he thought to himself, 'for then I might have seen Jesus for myself. But old John knew him well, and I can trust all he has told me about the Master.'

As he thought about the word 'Master', an idea flashed through Polycarp's mind.

'The night before I was sold, I promised Mum that I'd be a good slave to my new master. Little did I know that, one day, the best of all masters would call me into his service, and that I'd become a willing slave of the Lord God Almighty. He has called me to minister to his people here in Smyrna, and I'll do it to the very best of my ability.'

Many years later, the persecution of Christians became the sport of the day. Those who trusted in Jesus had been persecuted to a greater or lesser degree, ever since the Lord had risen from the dead, but it developed into a fine art. Polycarp watched as member after member of the church was targeted, and he knew that his day would probably come before long.

'I'm an old man anyway,' he thought. 'I'd rather they took me and left young energetic men to continue the Lord's work.'

Then one night, Polycarp had a dream, a dream he felt sure would come true. And in his dream he was burnt at the stake for being a Christian. He had just told his friends about his dream, when news spread that Roman soldiers were on the hunt for old Polycarp.

'Come away with us,' some church members insisted, as they hustled him off to a village near the town. 'We'll keep you safe.'

But they had no sooner arrived, than their bishop told them that he wasn't going to run away and hide, that he would face up to whatever was to happen to him.

Just three days after his dream, soldiers appeared in the village to which he'd been taken. Far from hiding away from them, the old man strode out to meet them and invited them in for a meal! Taken by surprise – and hungry as soldiers always are – they accepted the invitation and went in.

'May I pray while you eat?' Polycarp asked his captors.

They saw no harm in that, and for the next two hours the bishop prayed aloud to his Father in heaven. Some of the soldiers were so impressed by what he said in his prayer that they were uncomfortable about arresting him after all … not that their feelings made any difference to their orders. But they did try to make things easier for him.

'Just do what they say,' the kinder soldiers told him, when they arrived back in the city and put Polycarp into a chariot. 'Just agree that Caesar is god and offer a sacrifice to him. There's no harm in that, and if you do it, they'll release you and that will be an end of it.'

'I will not do what you want me to do,' the old man said firmly, much to the annoyance of his captors.

'I thought this one would be a walkover,' one soldier said to another.

His colleague shook his head. 'The old ones can be obstinate,' he muttered.

In a fit of mass fury, the crowd that had gathered to watch the spectacle threw Polycarp from the chariot. He landed on his side and badly injured his thigh. Seeing him lying there seemed to set the bloodthirsty crowd alight, and they screamed for his execution.

'You're an old man,' one of the judges said, in an effort to help. 'Just say you're sorry and deny that you believe in Jesus.'

'Eighty and six years have I now served Christ, and he has never done me the least wrong,' Polycarp told him. 'How then can I blaspheme my King and my Saviour?'

Again the judges tried to make him change his mind, but the old man's mind was not for changing.

That was it. Three times the judge called out to the crowd what Polycarp's crime was.

'He is a Christian, the leader of the Christians here, and he's an enemy of our gods. He has taught many people that they should not sacrifice to our gods or worship them.'

Sentence was passed.

'Take him to the stake and burn him alive.'

Polycarp nodded.

'So my dream is to come true after all,' he thought.

The old man was led away to be burned. But when the soldiers prepared to secure him to the stake before lighting the fire, he told them not to bother. 'Let me alone as I am,' he said. 'God will give me courage to stay in the fire. I won't move away.'

It was then that Polycarp stopped speaking to men and began speaking to God. Looking up to the heavens, he prayed aloud, thanking his heavenly Father for the privilege of being a martyr for Jesus Christ. And when he had finished praying, the executioner lit the fire.

When the Apostle John wrote the book of Revelation, God gave him these words: 'Be faithful to death, and I will give you a crown of life.' Seventy years after John wrote these words, Polycarp, who as a young man is said to have met the Apostle John, was faithful to death. And when he died and went to heaven, God kept his promise and gave him a crown of life.

Polycarp died not much more that 100 years after Jesus' death, which is a very long time ago. But papers from that time still exist, including some letters written by Polycarp himself, one written to him by another famous Christian martyr, and a brief account of his life written shortly after he died.

Fact File

Slavery: At the time that Polycarp lived in Smyrna, Turkey was known as the Province of Asia and was part of the Roman Empire. Slavery was a big part of the Roman economy, and the Romans viewed their slaves very differently from the way that we view people today. In the eyes of the law, slaves were not really people. They did not own anything themselves. All that they had was really owned by their master. In earlier times, the owner had the power of life and death over his slaves, although public authorities did more to control this by the time that Polycarp died.

Keynote: Polycarp was very scared about being sold to a new master and moving away from his mum and dad. It meant moving to a new place and leaving everyone he had ever known. However, God used it to place him with a much kinder master and to give him the chance to hear about Jesus. God is still the same. He can use situations that seem very scary, to work for our good and to give us more opportunity to serve him.

Think: Polycarp did not fight with the Roman soldiers when they came to arrest him. He followed Jesus' instruction to turn the other cheek instead (Matthew 5:39). This did not mean that Polycarp was a coward or ready to back down. He showed courage and loyalty, but not by fighting. Can you think of any situation where you can turn the other cheek and follow Jesus' and Polycarp's examples?

Prayer: Lord Jesus, thank you for caring for us and being with us wherever we are. Please help me to trust you in every situation and to be brave enough not to use violence. Amen.

Alban

Two boys climbed the earth bank that surrounded their town, then lowered themselves into the ditch beyond it.

'If I was leading an invasion, I'd bring my troops up the twenty miles from Londinium and then have them hide overnight, just a few miles south-west of Verulamium,' said Alban. 'Hiding them would give them time to regain their strength.'

'What would you do then?' asked his friend.

'I'd use diversionary tactics,' Alban explained. 'Like this.'

With a short stick the ten-year-old drew his plans on the summer-dry earth.

'See, here's the town with its earth bank surrounding it, and the deep ditch all round the outside of that. Away down there is Londinium.' (A long time later, Londinium changed its name to London).

The younger boy watched with interest as Alban worked it all out on the ground.

'Here is the river north-east of Verulamium. A small detachment of soldiers would leave the others resting, go due west till they reached the river where they would commandeer boats, making sure they tied up the people they'd taken them from, so that no one could raise the alarm. Then they'd row up river, silently in the darkness, until they were north-east of the town.'

'Why would you want most of your troops south-west of Verulamium and a detachment right at the opposite side of the town?'

Alban sat back on his heels.

'That's the trick,' he grinned. 'Before dawn broke, the detachment would act as though they were invading from the north-east, making as much noise and causing as much chaos as possible. The townsmen would rush to defend the town. And while they were all away on that wild goose chase, the main body of men would storm Verulamium from the south-west. They'd be down the ditch, up over the earth bank and in the town, before anyone knew what had happened.'

'That's a great plan!' the other boy laughed.

Alban looked serious. 'It could happen,' he said. 'If I were in charge of the Romans, I'd build a stone wall on top of the earth bank all the way round the city. It would be much safer then.'

'Maybe they'll think of that one day,' laughed his friend. 'And if they don't, you could study town planning and draw up the design for them.'

'I don't know if I'll be in Verulamium when I grow up,' Alban told his pal, as they walked. 'Father says that he's going to take me on his travels … and I might not come back.'

'Where are you going?' the other boy asked.

'We're going to the most exciting place in the world,' Alban laughed. 'In fact we're going right to the centre of the world!'

Alban's friend still couldn't guess.

'Father and I are going to reverse the Roman invasion. Instead of going from Rome to Verulamium, we're going to go from Verulamium to Rome.'

'Rome!' whispered the other lad. 'Will you go to see fights in the Colosseum, and chariots racing in the Circus Maximus? I heard one of the Roman soldiers say that, when it was built, the Circus Maximus could hold a quarter of a million people!' The boy looked at Alban and laughed. 'I suspect that if you go with your father, he's more likely to take you to the Roman Forum.'

'I think we'll do both,' said Alban. 'And if Dad spends too much time at the Roman Forum on business or listening to the politicians or worshipping in the temples, I'll remind him about the chariot races and suggest we head for the Circus Maximus.'

Alban did go to Rome. We don't know what he did there, but he most likely saw all the places he and his friend had talked about, and many more besides. Imagine him standing under the Trajan Column, and straining his head back as far as it would go to see the top. And think of him walking along the Via Sacra (the Sacred Way) to the temples where he and his father would worship the Roman gods. Perhaps he made an offering to the god Saturn in one of the most ancient temples in the whole of Rome for, like most people at the time of the Roman Empire, Alban and his family worshipped the Roman gods.

He was no sooner home from his travels when Alban met his old friend in Verulamium.

'I heard you were back,' the other lad said, 'and I was hoping to meet you. I'm really looking forward to hearing about your time in Rome.'

More than willing to talk on every aspect of the subject, Alban described fights in the Colosseum and chariot races in the Circus Maximus, and even the business and politics of the Roman Forum.

But his young friend could hardly wait for the story to finish.

'What do you think of Christians being thrown to the lions in the Colosseum?' he asked, hoping for some gory stories told in great detail.

Alban shook his head. 'I've met Christians,' he said, 'and they believe some very strange things. But I've never met one who seemed to do anything that deserved the death sentence.' The teenager shuddered. 'And certainly not to be killed by wild animals just to entertain Emperor Septimus Severus and the thousands of others who pay to get in.'

'So why are they thrown to the lions?' asked his friend.

'That's a great puzzle to me,' Alban replied. 'Because it's a terrible way to die.'

Alban grew up to be a fine young man. Because his family was wealthy, he was well known in Verulamium. But he was also respected for his own sake because he was kind and helpful. People who were in trouble felt able to go to Alban for help, even Christians. And there came a time in Verulamium when Christians certainly did need help, because Septimus Severus decided that Christians in Britain, as well as in Rome, should die if they would not give up their faith in the Lord Jesus Christ.

'Master,' Alban's servant said urgently, 'a man has arrived asking for your help. He says he's about to be arrested and killed.'

'Bring him to me immediately,' said Alban.

The servant was back within minutes, bringing with him an elderly man called Amphibalus.

'How can I help you?' Alban asked.

'My lord,' said Amphibalus, 'the Emperor's soldiers are searching for me.'

'Why?' asked the puzzled Alban, trying to imagine what terrible crime the old man could have committed.

'They are just following their orders,' Amphibalus explained. 'The Emperor Septimus Severus says that Christians should die.'

'Have you done wrong?' the young man asked, wanting to be quite sure.

'I have not broken the law of Rome,' said Amphibalus. 'My crime is that I am a Christian.'

'And how can I help you?'

'Hide me,' pleaded the old man. He looked round himself before saying, 'There is plenty of room here to hide me.'

'Fear nothing,' said Alban. 'I have heard a great deal about Christians, but nothing that is bad. You will be safe here.' And for a time he was, because the Roman soldiers didn't think to search a heathen's home to find a runaway Christian!

Every day that Amphibalus hid in Alban's house was a day of discovery for the young man. His fugitive told him the story of Jesus. Alban listened with interest. He knew about the Druid religion, and he knew about the Roman gods, but none were at all like Jesus.

'Tell me more,' Alban asked each day.

And Amphibalus told him more. He spoke of Jesus' birth in Bethlehem, of his teaching and stories. The young man was amazed at Jesus' miracles, and terribly saddened at the thought of his crucifixion.

'Three days after Jesus was crucified,' Amphibalus said one day, 'Jesus rose from the dead. His body was not in the tomb when his friends went to look for it.'

'You can imagine the search the Romans mounted for Jesus,' said the old man. 'It makes their search for me look like a children's game.'

'And did they find his body?' asked Alban.

'No, of course they didn't,' Amphibalus insisted. 'There was no body because Jesus Christ had risen from the dead; his spirit had returned to his body. He was not dead. He was gloriously alive ... and he still is.'

Alban was amazed and thrilled at what the old man was saying.

'Master!' said Alban's servant. 'They're here! The Roman soldiers have discovered about Amphibalus, and they've come to take him away.'

'My son,' said the old man. 'I must go now for I am about to die.'

'No,' Alban whispered, 'I think I can still save you.'

Amphibalus looked puzzled.

'Quickly, give me your robe,' urged Alban, as he took off his fine robe.

The two men exchanged robes, and stood looking at each other. Alban was wearing a simple, rough robe that was a little short for him, and Amphibalus had on a grand robe that was just a little too long for him.

'Take this,' whispered Alban.

Amphibalus looked down and saw that his young friend had pressed a purse of money into his hand.

'My servant will take you to safety by back roads, and I'll not give you away to the soldiers. Make the most of the time. Hurry now! And God go with you. But before you go,' said Alban, 'ask God to bless me.'

Kneeling down, Alban prayed with Amphibalus as the old man asked God to bless him.

'May God reward you for your kindness,' the Christian prayed. 'And may he lead you in the true way of Christ.'

Alban wrapped Amphibalus's robe around him, hitched the hood up over his head, and waited. The soldiers rushed into the room, saw a man dressed in the old Christian's clothes, and it never occurred to them to look under the hood to check who was there.

'Take him to the Governor!' the officer said, when the prisoner's wrists were tied together.

As he was marched along the roads of Verulamium, Alban might have detected an air of excitement in the soldiers who had captured him. The Emperor Septimus Severus had commanded that Christians in Britain should be killed, and now at last they had caught one and would carry out his command. That couldn't do their chances of promotion any harm!

Still with his hood round his head, the prisoner was led to the Roman Governor of Verulamium who was offering a sacrifice to one of his gods. Alban's wrists were loosened, and he raised his hand and pulled the hood off his head.

'What!' exclaimed the officer. 'That's not the Christian!'

'Get these soldiers out of here and punish them severely!' ordered the Governor, before turning his rage on Alban.

'How dare you help a Christian to escape!' he stormed. 'You know the Emperor's orders as well as I do. The Christian rebels have to be hunted out and killed if they won't give up their new beliefs!'

Alban stood with his head held high.

'Tell me where Amphibalus is hiding,' demanded the Governor. 'Then sacrifice to the gods to show them how sorry you are for what you've done.'

There was a minute of silence before Alban answered.

'I can do neither of these things,' he said quietly, but very firmly.

'Who do you think you are to defy me? What is your name?'

'My name is Alban.'

'Then, Alban,' said the Governor, trying to control himself, 'if you want the gods to forgive you, I suggest that you repent and make your sacrifices to them right away.'

'I cannot do that,' Alban told the official. 'I no longer believe in these gods. They teach people to be cruel and wicked. Amphibalus is the opposite. He is good and gentle, yet these gods tell the Emperor that he should be tortured and killed. I would rather believe in the God of Amphibalus. His teaching is that we love one another.'

In a fury, the Governor had Alban taken away, a condemned man.

Very soon afterwards, Alban, who had only been a Christian since his discussions with Amphibalus, was led out to a hillside to be executed. The news about what was to happen spread throughout Verulamium, and a great crowd gathered. Most were there because they were sorry that such a popular young man should be put to death for being such a fool. Although Alban was given every opportunity to deny his faith in Jesus, he did nothing of the sort. Just before he died, a remarkable thing happened. The soldier, whose job it was to behead him, wouldn't do it because he said that Alban was a good man.

'I would rather die than kill him,' the soldier bravely told his captain.

And he did. The captain first beheaded Alban, then he beheaded the soldier too.

Alban, who had been a Christian for just a few days, was not only the first martyr in Verulamium, he was the first Christian to die in Britain because he would not deny his faith in the Lord Jesus. Alban died for Jesus around 200 years after Jesus died on the cross for Alban, and for everyone else whose faith is in the Saviour.

Many years after Alban lived and died, his home town of Verulamium changed its name to St. Albans. And that's what it's known as today.

Fact File

Rome and Christianity: Roman emperors tended to be suspicious of Christians, but some were a lot fiercer than others. Perhaps the most notable was the Emperor Nero, who blamed Christians for a huge fire which nearly destroyed Rome and which some people believe he was responsible for himself. However, the persecution did not stop lots of people becoming Christians. By AD 313 the Roman Empire had split in two, and that year the two emperors, Constantine and Licinius agreed to stop persecuting the Christians.

Keynote: Amphibalus escaped because Alban took his place. We have all sinned, and this means that we deserve to be punished by God. However, Jesus has come to take our place so that we do not have to bear that punishment, if we put our trust in him.

Think: Alban wanted Amphibalus to pray for him because he could see that praying to God was not like praying to the Roman or Druid gods. Prayer to God really makes a difference because he has promised to hear us when we pray in Jesus' name. Think about who you could help by praying for them.

 Prayer: Lord Jesus, thank you for loving us so much that you came to take the punishment that we deserve. Help me to trust in you, so that I can have a special relationship with you and so that I can pray for those in need. Amen.

Sir John Oldcastle

'Left! Right! Left! Right!' said John, as he and his friend marched through Almeley in Herefordshire.

'Stop before the crossroads!' ordered his friend Walter. 'And dive for cover in case enemy forces are marching in from Leominster.'

The boys marched nearly to the crossroads that marked the centre of the village. Then they threw themselves down behind a hedge, before squirming right up to the junction, to check that the road in both directions was free of enemy action.

'All clear! Stand to attention!' barked John.

Walter scrambled to his feet.

'Quick march!'

The boys continued in step – at least they were in step after John double-hopped on his left foot to get into step with Walter.

'Now troops, straight to the castle!' yelled John. 'And duck under cover before you come to the ditch.'

The boys were as serious as though they were real soldiers. As soon as they neared the ditch that surrounded the castle mound, they were both on the ground squirming forward under cover of gorse bushes.

'We're nearly there,' Walter whispered. 'Another twenty feet and we'll be safe.'

Keeping as low to the ground as possible, and making no sound at all, other than the rustling of branches and the popping of gorse seedpods they disturbed along the way, they eventually reached their den, slid down the grassy slope into it and lay silently for a minute till they could be sure they'd not been followed.

'So what's the big secret?' Walter asked.

John had come for him earlier and had refused to explain the need for secrecy until they were in their den and absolutely sure they were alone.

'I heard my father talking to soldiers last night,' the boy whispered. 'He said that there was trouble in the Black Mountains, and that we'd to watch out for it spreading down in our direction.'

'What kind of trouble?' his friend wanted to know.

'Big trouble,' John explained. 'I don't know any more than that. But if it's from that direction, it could be more raids across the Welsh border. I got the impression that it was more serious than that. I think we should make plans to do undercover surveillance, and, if we see anything unusual, I can tell Dad.'

'What's surveillance?' asked Walter.

John put on an intelligent expression, much like his tutor did when he was asked a question to which he knew the answer.

'It's what soldiers do when they go spying on the enemy. From their hiding-places they spy out the enemy and take the information they gather to their commanding officer, who decides what to do about it.'

But as there didn't seem to be any urgent surveillance to be done, the two boys discussed soldiering in general, and John's future plans in particular.

'Are you really going to be a full-time soldier?' Walter asked. 'I thought your father might want you to do something else, and that's why he was having you educated.'

'Soldiers need an education too,' insisted John. 'And that's what I'm going to be. I've never wanted to do anything else. What about you?'

Walter grinned. 'I'll be a soldier if the king asks your father to raise an army from around these parts, but in between wars I'll be a miller like Dad.'

'The world needs millers as well as soldiers,' John laughed. 'When I come back from the wars, I'll enjoy bread made from flour you've milled.'

John did become a professional soldier, and a good one too. He fought in France and made such an impression on his officers that he was given a knighthood. Enter SIR John Oldcastle! And in 1406 he was awarded a pension of £40 a year – a fortune in those days. Back from the army, John had time for other interests. One thing especially interested him, and he discussed this with his friend Walter, as they walked from his home to the mill one day.

Taking a small sheet of paper from his pocket, John held it out to Walter.

'Look at that,' he said, with almost a sense of reverence in his voice.

'What is it?' asked Walter.

John explained that it was paper, paper with writing on it.

'I've never seen paper before,' his friend said. 'Dad says that by the beginning of next century, most homes will have paper in them. But I've never seen any before.'

'We have books at home, but this paper's rather special.'

'You've only got books because your dad's Sir Richard Oldcastle of Almeley. My dad's just a miller. In any case, why's this bit special?'

'Do you want to know what the writing says?' John asked, exasperated that Walter hadn't asked. 'I'll read it to you.'

Walter held the scrap of paper in his hand as carefully as he might have held a bird's egg. John leant over his shoulder, cleared his throat, and read.

'And Jhesus, seynge the puple, wente vp in to an hil; and whanne he was set, hise disciplis camen to hym.

And he openyde his mouth, and tauyte hem, and seide,

Blessed ben pore men in spirit, for the kyngdom of heuenes is herne.

Blessid ben mylde men, for thei schulen welde the erthe.

Blessid ben thei that mornen, for thei schulen be coumfortid.

Blessid ben thei that hungren and thristen riytwisnesse, for thei schulen be fulfillid.

Blessid ben merciful men, for thei schulen gete merci.

Blessid ben thei that ben of clene herte, for thei schulen se God.

Blessid ben pesible men, for thei schulen be clepid Goddis children.

Blessid ben thei that suffren persecusioun for riytfulnesse, for the kingdam of heuenes is herne.'

(Matthew 5:1-10)

39

'That's from the Bible,' explained John.

'You can read Latin and say the words in English at the same time!' Walter gasped. He'd no idea his friend was so well educated.

'No,' John said. 'That's not written in Latin. The words Jesus said are written in English. They're from Mr Wycliffe's translation of the Bible into English.'

Walter's face drained of its colour.

'Where did you get that?' he whispered, though there wasn't anyone within a quarter of a mile.

John shrugged. 'It's best you don't know. What you don't know, you can't tell, even if you're tortured.'

Handing the paper back to his friend, Walter announced he'd have to go.

'I'm not sure when I'll be able to see you again. And you be careful who you show that to.'

John watched his friend disappearing. He bit his lip in thought.

'Maybe I shouldn't have shown him it,' he thought. 'Maybe that was a stupid thing to do.'

Mr John Wycliffe and his friends translated the whole Bible verse by verse into English. Printing presses had not been invented, and the whole thing was done by hand. As each section was translated, it was copied, again by hand, then the copies were copied, then the copies of the copies were copied, then the copies of the copies of the copies were copied! You get the idea? The next time Walter had the courage to meet his friend, this was their topic of conversation.

'Did you tell anyone what I showed you?' John asked.

Walter shook his head. 'But I asked my dad about that Mr Wycliffe. He said the man is a menace!'

'What else did he say?' his friend asked quietly.

'He said that the priests are angry that Mr Wycliffe translated the Bible into English, because they don't want ordinary people to read it. Dad says that if ordinary people read the Bible, we won't need priests, and they'd all be out of a job!'

John smiled at the thought. 'Did your dad tell you that what the priests teach is often not in the Bible at all? And the priests are scared that people will read the Bible for themselves and discover that.'

'No,' Walter said. 'Is that true?'

Nodding his head, John gave an example.

'The priests say that, when we die, we go to Purgatory, don't they?'

His friend shivered at the thought. 'And we will only get out of there if those who are still alive pray for our souls and give money to the priests.'

'Well,' John said triumphantly. 'That's not in the Bible. Mr Wycliffe says that the Bible teaches that everyone who believes in the Lord Jesus Christ and asks him to forgive their sins, goes to heaven. There's no such place as Purgatory!'

For a minute, Walter's face lit up, then he looked really scared.

'I wish that was true,' he said, 'for I'm scared stiff of Purgatory. What if there's nobody left to pray for me after I die? I'll end up being there forever.'

'But there's no such place,' John insisted. 'Mr Wycliffe and his friends finished their translation work twenty years ago. Now we can all read the Bible and discover for ourselves if what the Church teaches is true or not.'

Walter shook his head. 'No way,' he said. 'If the priests found out, there'd be trouble. In any case, I can't read.'

John Oldcastle studied Mr Wycliffe's Bible and knew in his heart it was true. He became a Christian and was baptised in a stream near his home. He married Joan in 1408, and, through her, he inherited the title Lord Cobham. It wasn't long before his name changed again, but not everyone agreed with the new one. John was known among Christians as Good Lord Cobham, though there were many who thought he was far from good, mostly priests and followers of the Roman Church. Those who called him Good Lord Cobham were Lollards, men like John Wycliffe, who read the Bible for themselves and knew the church of their day was in error.

'What a busy house we have,' Joan laughed, 'if there's not someone coming, someone has just left.'

John looked at his wife and smiled. 'You're very patient with all our visitors. And it's part of a wonderful work.'

'Tell me exactly what we're involved in,' she said. 'I'm sure there are things going on that I don't really understand.'

It was evening, the fire was blazing in the huge fireplace, and the candles were dancing in their holders. John Oldcastle was relaxed and happy, especially as his wife had recently had a little boy whom they'd called Henry.

'We're so privileged,' he said. 'We have a big house and no money worries. And we have the glorious gospel of Jesus Christ to give us hope, for time and for eternity.'

Joan looked at her little boy and hoped that, one day, he too would be a Christian.

'There are many in England and Wales who are still being misled by Romanist priests. They are imprisoned by the fact they don't have access to the Bible, in which they can find the truth that would set them free. That's why I'm happy that our home is used for travelling preachers of the truth, and for those who want to come to study the Bible here.'

'How safe is what we're doing?' Joan asked.

'We're safe as long as Henry IV is on the throne, as we've been friends since he was Prince of Wales. How safe we'll be if he dies, I really don't know.'

In 1413 that's just what happened. Henry IV died, and his son, Henry V, became king. The Roman Church leaders, who knew perfectly well what John was doing, decided that the time had come to act, even if they had to lie to have him arrested.

'I'm charged with what?' Sir John asked the soldiers who came to arrest him.

'You're charged with being involved in an illegal uprising,' he was told.

Before his friends could get organised to help him, John was locked up in the Tower of London. As he looked out of the window to the river Thames and thought of the Welsh hills, he made plans to get back there. Even when they were boys, Walter was impressed by his friend's ability to make military plans; he was even more impressed by his escape from the Tower of London when he heard about it. All John's training stood him in good stead for travelling in secret, and he was soon reunited with his wife and baby son. The authorities were furious at what had happened, and a warrant was put out for his arrest.

It was three years before the authorities caught up with John again, and when they did, they made sure he could not escape from the Tower a second time. In December 1417, Good Lord Cobham was taken before Parliament where he was found guilty of heresy and treason.

'What will happen to him now?' his friends asked each other.

And they watched as he was put on to a wooden hurdle and drawn through the streets of London to St Giles Fields. What happened to him there was unspeakable; sufficient is it to say that he was horribly tortured before being burned to death.

'He thought his money would save him,' the priests said to one another. 'But we got him in the end.'

John was a wealthy man, but his greatest treasure of all was not on earth but in heaven. When he died and went there, Jesus welcomed him home.

The verses John read from the Bible are exactly as they were written in Mr Wycliffe's translation. And as Mr Wycliffe wanted people to be able to read the Bible in the language they normally used, we must assume that's how Sir John Oldcastle spoke.

FACT FILE

Translations of the Bible: The translation that John showed his friend was not a translation from the original languages. Instead, it was translated from a Latin version of the Bible called the Vulgate. This translation was originally meant for ordinary people. It was called the 'Vulgate' because it was written in the common language. (At that time the word vulgar meant common rather than rude). By the 1400s, however, very few people could read Latin so the Vulgate was not doing its job, and a translation into English was needed. In later years, translations made directly from the original languages appeared.

Keynote: Walter was afraid of Purgatory because the priests had told him about it. He was too scared to read the Bible for himself to find that it said nothing about Purgatory. If we do not look at the Bible for ourselves, we can be very easily misled because we can't check if things are right or not. Now we all have an opportunity to read the Bible without fear of persecution. But if we don't take it, we will be just the same as Walter was.

Think: When John spoke to his wife, he was very thankful for all the good things that God had given him. The thing that he was most grateful for was having heard the gospel so that he could believe in Jesus. Because he wanted to make sure that others could do the same, he helped preachers even when it put him in danger. Think of all of the good things that you have been given and how you can use them to serve God and to help others.

Prayer: Lord Jesus, thank you for letting me hear about all that you have done. Please help me to listen carefully when I am taught about you, and to read the Bible for myself. Please bless those people who are still translating the Bible into many languages around the world. Amen.

Thomas Cranmer

Thomas was the middle of the three boys standing on the bridge over the river, that ran through the small village of Aslacton. Each was holding a beech leaf as far over the side of the bridge as he could, and all were waiting for their mother to give the word.

'Go!' she said, and laughed as the boys dropped their leaves into the river then dashed to the other side of the bridge to see which one came through first.

'Mine doesn't have a stalk!' said Thomas.

But as the first leaf floated through – minus its stalk – his brothers said in unison, 'Neither does mine!'

Mrs Cranmer laughed. 'In that case, a very funny thing happened midstream, as the two leaves that are floating through now both have stalks on them. It seems that there's mischief going on under the bridge, because someone is sitting under there sticking stalks on to leaves that have lost theirs, just to confuse the game.'

Thomas's brothers looked a little shamefaced.

'Let's play again,' said one.

'Only if you work out which is which beforehand,' Mrs Cranmer suggested.

'Mine doesn't have a stalk,' Thomas pointed out.

'One side of mine is yellow,' one brother said.

'And mine has a nick out of it,' announced the other.

The game was played once again, and Thomas's stalkless leaf won fair and square.

'The three of you are so competitive,' complained Mrs Cranmer, as they walked the short distance from the bridge to their home. 'If you're out with your bows and arrows, you've always got to be better than each other, and it's the same when you're riding the horses. Sometimes I wake up in the night dreaming that you're all shouting at each other, "I won! I won!"'

'But I did win this time,' laughed Thomas.

Mrs Cranmer shook her head. 'I don't know what I'll do with you all, if it's not knocking your heads together to put some sense into them!'

The boys realised that they'd wound their mother up quite enough for one day, and that if they went much further they might find themselves doing some horrible chores when they got home.

'Is Squire Cranmer at home?' a man asked, as they reached their house door.

'I don't rightly know,' said Mrs Cranmer, 'I'm just coming home myself. Wait for a minute and I'll see.'

Bustling into the house, she left the boys to chat to the man.

'Have you come far?' asked Thomas. 'You don't sound as though you come from Nottinghamshire.'

'No, young sir,' the man replied. 'I've come from over the English Channel. My master sent me to Nottingham and said that I'd to visit Squire Cranmer before my return.'

Thomas' father came rushing out of the door to see who the stranger was. One look from their father and the boys knew that they'd best be off and leave the men in peace. That was no hardship as they went round the back of the house to their shooting range, set up a target and had a competition with their longbows. But the visitor was no sooner away than all three boys tumbled into the house to find out all they could about him.

'Who was that?' they asked their father, all at once.

Mr Cranmer was smiling. 'He works for a distant relation of ours.'

'But I thought he was French,' said the oldest boy. 'He said he'd come from over the English Channel.'

'So did your many-times-great-grand-father,' Mr Cranmer reminded his sons. 'Don't you forget your heritage. One of your forebears came over the English Channel with William the Conqueror and landed in Hastings before heading north for the great battle, that shaped English history from that day to this.'

'But that was hundreds of years ago,' said Thomas.

'This is the year 1499, so it was 433 years ago, and landed families have long memories.'

The next day, Thomas discovered the ideal way of distracting his teacher from Latin.

'Please Mr Morice,' he said. 'Father says our family came to England with William the Conqueror in 1066, and I wondered if you could tell us more about that conquest.'

'Yes, please,' said his brothers, one after the other.

Ralph Morice smiled at his pupils' sudden interest in history and was more than happy to oblige. For three boys who had just realised their roots, it took on a whole new meaning. Thomas thought long and hard about his family history and decided that 1066 was a long time ago, and that he was a true Englishman, and the English king was his king.

Just a short time later, the three boys were glad that they'd listened to their father tell the family story, because Mr Cranmer died, and it might have gone to the grave with him.

In 1503, when Thomas was fourteen years old, he left Aslacton (now spelt Aslockton) and went to Cambridge University to study. Mr Morice must have been proud of his former pupil because he did very well indeed. Seven years later, he became a Fellow of Jesus College, and it looked as though he had settled down to a quiet academic life. It was there that he discovered that his many-times-great-grandfather was not the only good thing that came over the Channel from Europe, because, in the first half of the 15th Century, new thinking was finding its way into Cambridge from various parts of Europe, and Thomas was not slow to find out what it was.

'I must think,' Thomas said to himself, as he walked along the River Cam. 'I need peace to think.'

Mallards paddled their way along the river, stopping from time to time to do a bottoms-up, all the better to catch their dinner. Sometimes the sight of them amused Dr Cranmer, but not today. His mind was on weightier things.

'If what the European Reformers say is right, then the Roman Church is wrong. And if the Roman Church is wrong, then ... then what?'

And as his thinking ground to a halt, he noticed the mallards. 'It's all right for them,' he thought. 'They know what they're looking for, and they puddle about till they find it.'

Leaving the mallards behind him, he walked on. A few strides further along the way, he turned back to look at the ducks. 'You're right,' he told them. 'And I'm going to follow your example. I know what I'm looking for; I'm looking for the truth. And I'm going to puddle about till I find it.'

Cranmer studied three things: his Bible, the Roman Church and the teaching of the European Reformers. It took time, but eventually he came to the conclusion that what the Reformers taught was the same as the Bible, and much of what the Roman Church taught at that time was not. Thomas was not the only one who was thinking along these lines; the King of England was coming to the same conclusion, though he travelled along a different route to arrive there. Both men were leaving their Roman faith behind them and becoming Protestant in their thinking.

For Thomas the issues were theological. That's a big word, but here's a 100-word outline of the issues that helped him make up his mind. The Roman Church said that the Communion bread and wine were really the body and blood of Jesus; the Reformers (and the Bible) said they were symbols. The Roman Church thought people could buy their way into heaven by giving money to the Church;

the Reformers (and the Bible) said that we are saved by faith in Jesus. The Roman Church believed that people had to approach God through priests or dead saints; the Reformers (and the Bible) said that everyone could come to God through Jesus. And the Roman Church didn't like people reading the Bible, whereas the Reformers did. Oops! That's 101 words! King Henry VIII came to the problem from quite a different angle. He wanted to divorce his wife; and the Pope, who was head of the Roman Church, would not agree to it.

'I think that I'll move from Cambridge for the summer,' Thomas told a friend in 1529. 'There's such a lot of illness here just now that getting away seems a good idea.'

His friend agreed, and Cranmer made plans to spend some months in Waltham, Essex. While he was there he met two men, Edward Fox and Stephen Gardiner. That meeting was to change the course of Cranmer's life. Fox and Gardiner were advisors to King Henry VIII, and if there was one thing he needed a lot of, it was advice. Cranmer's new friends decided that he was just the person to advise the king, and arranged for the two men to meet. Four years later, in 1533, Cranmer was appointed Archbishop of Canterbury, which really meant that he was head of the newly born Protestant church in England.

Cranmer remained one of Henry VIII's chief advisers for as long as the king lived.

'It's not always easy,' Thomas confided in his best friend. 'I certainly don't agree with all the king does and says, although people think I do because I'm Archbishop of Canterbury. But sometimes the Archbishop's throne is not a comfortable seat to be sitting on.'

Thinking of King Henry's six wives, Thomas's friend was quite sure that what Cranmer said was true.

'I'm sure you advise him well, even when you don't agree with him,' the man decided.

Cranmer said nothing, but he wondered if what his friend said was right.

'My main job is not what I do to support the King,' Thomas said. 'My job is to try to establish a Protestant church in England, a church that is founded on what the Bible teaches rather than on men's traditions. That's my job. And the part of it that's keeping me busy just now is compiling a prayer book. I believe that if people don't have a Protestant Prayer Book, they'll go back to their old Roman prayers. And before they realise what they're doing, they'll be praying to God through the saints once again, rather than through the Lord Jesus.'

If Thomas thought life would be easier after Henry VIII died, he was very much mistaken. Henry's son Edward VI, who was a Protestant like his father, reigned for just a short time then died. His sister Mary, who should have succeeded him, was Roman Catholic. Henry VIII had wanted his relation, Lady Jane Grey, to succeed his son, as she too was a Protestant. When Edward VI died, Cranmer supported Lady Jane Grey's claim to the throne. She reigned for just over a week before Mary was proclaimed queen. And the next thing Cranmer knew was that he was charged with treason and thrown into the Tower of London with a death sentence hanging over his head. It was not carried out.

Four years later, Queen Mary had Thomas Cranmer charged with heresy for his Protestant teaching. Once again he was sentenced to death, this time by burning.

'Can we make him deny his Protestant teaching?' the Queen's advisers asked each other. 'We could tell him that his life would be spared, that he would remain as Archbishop. In fact, we could promise him the moon on a plate if it would make him change his mind.'

Cranmer was brought before them. Brainwashing over his years in prison had taken its toll on him, and he was a greatly weakened man. Promises were made to him, false promises, if only he'd deny his Protestant faith. In the terrible stress of the situation, Thomas Cranmer did what the

Queen most wanted. He agreed that what the Roman Church taught was true.

'Do you agree that the Pope is head of the church?' he was asked.

'I do.'

'Do you agree that the bread and wine are the actual body and blood of Jesus?'

'I do.'

'Sign your name to it!' he was told.

And taking the quill pen in his right hand, he dipped it in ink and signed away the truth.

If Thomas Cranmer thought his signature would save his life, he was wrong. The sentence of death still stood. And when the day came for his burning, a terrible sermon was preached to him, and questions were asked to show the onlookers that the famous Reformer wasn't a Reformer at all, but that he'd gone back to his old Roman faith.

'Master Cranmer,' the preacher said, 'tell all the people what you truly believe.'

'I will,' said the former Archbishop. 'I believe in God the Father Almighty. And I believe every word taught by our Saviour Jesus Christ, and his apostles.'

There was a moment of silence before he went on. 'And now I come to the great thing' he said, his voice growing stronger as he went on. 'For fear of death I signed my name to lies. As for the Pope, I refuse him. He is Christ's enemy!'

The soldiers could hardly believe their ears.

'And the bread and the wine are just that, bread and wine, pictures of the body and blood of Christ, not the real thing.'

The crowd yelled at him for his heresy, and screamed for him to be burned.

Cranmer held up his right hand. 'This hand,' he shouted above the noise, 'this hand, with which I put my name to such lies, will burn first in the fire that will kill me.'

Which is exactly what happened. So ashamed was he of what he had done, when he signed that sheet of paper, Thomas held out his hand to the flames and watched as they lapped around it. Having done something he was desperately ashamed of, Thomas Cranmer went to his death in the sure knowledge that all his sins, even his denial of his Protestant faith, were confessed and forgiven through the Lord Jesus Christ.

FACT FILE

Henry's daughters: When she succeeded to the throne, Mary soon began trying to overturn the reforms to the church that had been put in place during her father's reign, and that of her brother. She executed so many Protestants that she was given the nickname 'Bloody Mary'. However, the changes that she put in place did not last long because she was succeeded by her half-sister, Elizabeth, who was a Protestant, and who regarded Catholics as a threat to the safety of the kingdom. Elizabeth put many of the reforms made by her father back in place, although this brought her into conflict with countries on the continent of Europe.

Keynote: Thomas made a big mistake when he lied about what he believed in an attempt to escape execution. He did something wrong, and it did not do him any good. In the end wrong things we do, don't help us as we think they will. However, Thomas did something about it by admitting that what he had done was wrong and renouncing it. God does not want us to be paralysed by wrong things that we have done in the past. He wants us to ask his forgiveness and to deal with them, with his help.

Think: Thomas knew it was very important for people to realise that Jesus was the only way to God the Father. There was no need to pray through saints. It is a great privilege to be able to pray to God in Jesus' name. Jesus teaches us in God's Word to pray to God as Father. The first part of the Lord's Prayer is 'Our Father, hallowed be your name.' Think about how God is the perfect and best father you could ever have. What does this mean? The word hallowed means - to give honour to and bless. How can you give honour to God's name? How can you glorify him?

Prayer: Lord Jesus, thank you for coming and dying so that we can have forgiveness for our sins. Please forgive me for the bad things that I have done. and give me the courage to face up to them. Amen.

George Wishart

George watched from the window of his home at Pitarrow, in that part of Scotland that was then called Forfarshire. He was searching the road to the south for any signs of his uncle's arrival.

'Will Uncle James be here soon?' he asked his mother. 'I seem to have been watching for ages.'

Mrs Wishart smiled. She too was looking forward to her brother's visit but, unlike her son, she realised that watching from the window would not bring him any more quickly. She was especially glad that he was coming, because since her husband died, she felt the lack of a man's guidance on her young son's life.

'I think I can see him coming!' the boy yelled from his perch at the window. 'I'm sure that's his carriage coming now!'

But it was another false alarm, the fourth that afternoon, for many people travelled the road from Brechin to Stonehaven.

'Wait until you see one turning left into Pitarrow,' said Mrs Wishart, who was beginning to tire of the lad's excitement.

'There he is!' George shouted triumphantly, 'and there's no mistake. His carriage is bumping up our road right now!'

Mother and son were at the door in a flash, and it was hard to say who was the more excited.

'This afternoon is all yours, young man,' James Learmont told his nephew the next morning. 'And all I ask is that we get out into the fresh air together. You choose what we do and where we go.'

As soon as their lunch was eaten, uncle and nephew made for the door.

'Where are we going?' James Learmont asked.

'We're going on my favourite walk and to my special place,' was all George would tell him.

Leaving Pitarrow, they turned west and followed the course of the stream that flowed past the house. It took a sharp right turn almost immediately, then swung left again half a mile later.

'Are we going up the hill?' asked Uncle James.

George nodded. 'The stream starts not far from the top of the hill, and we'll follow it up. Then we'll climb to the top of the hill; it's called Finella Hill. It's not high, but there's a wonderful view.'

James Learmont sat down at the hilltop and looked around.

'You're right, young man,' he said. 'You can see a fair distance from here.'

George stretched his arm out and turned in a circle, telling his uncle the names of the hills all around. 'That's Sturdy Hill to the west, then Cairn o' Mount in the north, and that's the Goyle Hill to the right of it. When he'd turned full circle, he was pointing east, to the sea that shone blue just a few miles from where they sat.

'One day I'll cross the sea,' he said. 'But I'll have to wait a while because I can't leave Mum on her own.'

Mr Learmont caught an edge in George's voice and decided to ask what he knew might upset his nephew.

'Are you missing your dad terribly?' he asked quietly.

The boy nodded.

'Tell me about him,' George said, after a few minutes of silence. 'There are so many things I wish I'd asked before he died, and now I can't.'

Uncle James wondered where to begin.

'You know your dad was a lawyer, but you probably don't know much more about that. His title was Clerk of Justiciary and

King's Advocate, which means he was a very important person indeed.'

'I thought he must have been important,' the lad said. 'He kept having private meetings with people, and he was away a lot.'

'What you may not know,' his uncle went on, 'was that your mother – my sister – was your dad's second wife. His first wife died very young.'

George nodded. 'I wondered about that.'

'What else do you want to know?' James Learmont asked.

But George had had enough. He knew his uncle was staying for a week, which would give him time to find out more.

'You said you wanted to go away one day,' said James, as they climbed back down Finella Hill. 'I hope you will, because that's part of your education. Another thing, don't worry about your mother. She's able to look after herself, and I'll do all I can to help her.'

That was like a burden off George's back. He grinned at his uncle and said that he'd leave for Aberdeen that afternoon to book a voyage round the world!

When the time came for George to go to university, he did go overseas. It was while he was studying in Europe that he came in contact with the Reformers. For it was the 16th Century, and the Christian church was in turmoil. Young Master Wishart discovered that new thinking was spreading from village to village and town to town. Like most young people, George was interested in what was new, and he became very interested indeed when he found out more.

'Let me get this straight,' he said to his university friends. 'You're telling me that what the Roman Church teaches is very different from the Bible.'

'That's often the case.'

'So where does the Church's teaching come from if it's not from the Bible?'

The young men looked around to see who would answer. It was a German lad who did.

'The fact is that much of the Church's teaching comes from traditions that go back hundreds of years. Other things just seem to be taken on board to suit the Church's convenience.'

'Like what?' asked George.

'Like indulgences,' said his German friend. 'There's not a word about indulgences in the Bible. But when the Church needs money for some big project, it sells sheets of paper called indulgences that are meant to help those who buy them get in to heaven. It seems to me that has more to do with money than truth.'

'Don't take our word for it,' a student from Switzerland advised. 'Read the Bible yourself and make up your own mind about what is true.'

One of George's subjects was New Testament Greek, and he put it to very good use. It was not long before he was a convinced Reformer, one of the early Protestants. (Protestants protested against the teaching of the Roman Church.)

When George returned to Scotland in 1534 to become a Greek teacher in a school in Montrose, he brought with him copies of the New Testament in Greek for his pupils. He also brought a copy of the Helvetic Confession (an outline of Protestant teaching) that he had translated into English.

'Will you find a nice home for yourself in Montrose?' Mrs Wishart asked, when George travelled the twenty or so miles to Pitarrow for a visit. 'You mustn't worry about money,' she went on. 'The family is well set up, so you'll never have to do without anything.'

'I need nothing grand,' the young man explained. 'I have very simple tastes.'

And it was a very simple life indeed that the teacher decided to follow. He lived in humble lodgings, ate only twice a day, and every fourth day he hardly ate anything at all. None of these things were done to save money – George had no need to do that – rather they were done as disciplines he set on himself.

George Wishart, however, was not destined to spend his life teaching Greek to the boys of Montrose. In 1538, the fact that he was teaching his pupils to read the Bible in the original language – or to read it at all – came to the attention of the Church authorities, and he had to leave Scotland for Cambridge. The story of Wishart's life is very confusing; as some history books tell us, he studied in Aberdeen as a young man, then went to the continent after teaching in Montrose; others assure us that he was in Europe first, then went to Cambridge from Montrose! However, we do know that he was in Cambridge by 1543, because John Foxe (who wrote a famous book about Christian martyrs) met him there. So although there is some confusion about George's life, we do have a good description of what he looked like. Funny thing, history!

Foxe tells us, 'About the year of our Lord 1543, there was in the University of Cambridge, one Master George Wishart … a man of tall stature, polled-headed, and on the same a round French cap of the best; judged to be of melancholy complexion, black-haired, long-bearded, comely of personage, well spoken after his country of Scotland, courteous, lowly, lovely, glad to teach, desirous to learn and well travelled.' We even know the kind of clothes he wore! 'Having on him for his clothing a frieze gown to the shoes, a black millian fustian doublet, and plain black hosen, coarse new canvass for his shirts, and white falling bands and cuffs at his hands.'

By the following year, Wishart was back in Scotland, preaching the good news of Jesus Christ at every opportunity, and making himself mightily unpopular with the Roman Church. His life was so much in danger that he travelled with a bodyguard, one John Knox, who became Scotland's most famous reformer. It is impossible to state how important Wishart was in the Scottish Reformation, because not only did he preach in many towns and cities, his influence continued through Knox, whose life was changed by Wishart's ministry.

'You can't go preaching where the plague's raging,' a friend told Wishart.

'The plague I preach against is Romanist teaching,' George said. 'As for preaching where the plague is, I can think of no better place. There are people there who will shortly die, and I must tell them to look to Jesus for forgiveness before they do. Otherwise they'll die looking to the Church's teachings and with no hope of heaven.'

'I can't argue with that,' his friend agreed. 'And I'll pray for you and those who hear you preach.'

Hard on Wishart's heels was the most important Romanist in Scotland, Cardinal Beaton. He disliked George Wishart with a passion, and was determined to silence his preaching whatever it took to do that.

On one occasion, Wishart was about to set out to preach in Montrose, when a message arrived from a friend saying that he had taken ill and needed George to visit right away. He prepared to go immediately, and some friends agreed to travel with him for the first part of the journey. They had hardly gone quarter of a mile, when George Wishart reined his horse to a standstill.

'I am forbidden by God to go on this journey,' he said. 'Will some of you be pleased to ride to yonder place (he pointed to a nearby hill) and see what you find, for I see there is a plot against my life?'

Turning his horse round, he rode off in the direction from which he had come. It wasn't long before his friends joined him, with the news that sixty horsemen had been waiting to ambush him, and the letter from his sick friend was a forgery written to draw him into the trap.

'God has spared me this time,' said George. 'This time.'

The more Reformation teaching spread throughout Scotland, the more viciously Cardinal

Beaton tried to stamp it out, and that meant stamping out those who preached it. As others were martyred before him, Wishart no doubt knew what was coming. It would have come as no surprise to him when he was captured and thrown into prison in St Andrews. His Cambridge friend, John Foxe, was not in St Andrews in March 1546 when George was martyred, but he no doubt heard the details from those who were. Foxe records what happened when George was hanged and burnt.

'When he came to the fire, he sat down upon his knees, and rose again, and three times he said these words, 'O thou Saviour of the world! have mercy on me. Father of heaven! I commend my spirit into Thy holy hands.' ... Then he turned to the crowd who had gathered to watch him die, and said to them, 'I suffer this day by men, not sorrowfully, but with a glad heart and mind. For this cause I was sent, that I should suffer this fire, for Christ's sake. Consider and behold my face; you shall not see me change my colour. This grim fire I fear not. I know surely that my soul shall sup with my Saviour Christ this night.'

The hangman, who saw and heard what was happening, knelt down before Wishart and said, 'Sir, I pray you forgive me, for I am not guilty of your death.'

'Come here to me,' George said. And when the man came within reach, George Wishart kissed him.

'That is a token that I forgive you,' he said. 'Do your job.'

The forgiven executioner did his job. He hanged the young preacher and lit the fire below him. Cardinal Beaton watched from the window of St Andrews Castle and thought that was the end of George Wishart. How wrong he was. It was a glorious new beginning. For, as Beaton watched the flames die down, George was beginning eternity in the presence of Jesus.

FACT FILE

Continental travel: George Wishart was not the only Scots preacher to return from university in Europe with new ideas. Many of the Scottish reformers had travelled widely in Europe and were influenced, in particular, by the teachings of John Calvin, a Frenchman who had moved to Geneva. Many Protestants fled to Geneva to escape persecution in other parts of Europe. Geneva seems to have influenced George's clothes as well as his religion, since the white bands that Foxe describes were later referred to as Geneva bands.

Keynote: George was not a poor man, but he still lived a very simple life because he wanted to discipline himself and avoid being distracted from what was really important. He was willing to set aside many comforts, and even risk being infected with the plague, for the sake of telling people the gospel and making sure that they knew what the Bible actually said. We must be careful that the comforts of this life do not take our attention away from trying to please God.

Think: George was not afraid to die because he knew that when he died, he would go to heaven to be with Jesus. That helped him to be very brave when he was about to be executed. He was even able to forgive his executioner! He knew that everything was in God's hands. What difference does knowing that everything is in God's hands make to the way you react, when things go wrong or when sad things happen?

 Prayer: Lord Jesus, thank you for giving people in the past the courage to stand up for what the Bible really said, so that we can read it now. Please help me to follow you, even when other people make that very difficult. Amen.

James Chalmers

'When do I start school?' the boy asked his mother. 'How many days is it till I go?'

Mrs Chalmers smiled and wondered if her son would be as keen to go to school every day after he'd discovered what it was like.

'You start school next Monday,' she said. 'And you'll work hard when you go there.'

James grinned. The thought of his first day at school made him feel very grown up, even though he wasn't yet six years old. Despite his excitement, he was more than a little nervous when Monday dawned, and he pulled on his scratchy school jersey and tucked his slate under his arm.

'Beat him if he needs it,' Mrs Chalmers told the teacher, before leaving the boy that Monday.

That gave James a little cause for concern. 'Does Mum expect me to be beaten on my very first day?' he wondered.

James' slate had fine white lines drawn on it. With a scratchy slate pencil, he was taught to write the letters of the alphabet within the lines. And even quite small boys were punished when the tops of their letters went above the lines, or the bottoms of the letters went below them. After the slate was covered with trial letters, they were rubbed out with a damp rag, and the whole process started all over again. Not only that, James had to carry his slate home to practise even more letters. There were many things he would rather be doing.

'Where are you working today?' the boy asked his father, one fine Saturday morning.

'I've some work to do on the prison walls,' Mr Chalmers told his son. 'It seems that the rain's dripping into one of the cells, and the authorities don't want their prisoners wet.'

'May I come with you?' James asked.

'I don't see why not. You're not likely to run away from the inside of Inveraray Prison, are you?'

James laughed at the thought.

'I'll be able to tell the boys at school that I was in jail on Saturday,' thought James. 'But I'd better not tell the teacher. He might think I was there for real.'

So Mr Chalmers and James set off to walk to the prison. James carried their lunch wrapped in a cloth, and his father had a much heavier load: a jute sack with all his stonemason's hammers and chisels inside it.

'Look at the fishing boats on Loch Fyne,' the lad said, when they came out of the trees into the village. 'I wonder if they'll get a good catch today.'

'Did you know that not all boats have red-brown sails like these ones?' asked his father.

'No,' said James. 'What other colours are there?'

Mr Chalmers explained that the Loch Fyne boats were a special kind, and that most fishing boats in other places had lighter coloured sails, and that they were a different shape too.

'How do you know that?' asked the lad.

His father smiled. 'I know that because I was brought up in Aberdeen where there are hundreds of fishing boats. The fish market there is so huge that it makes the one in Inveraray look like a toy.'

'Did Mum come from Aberdeen too?' James enquired.

'No,' his father said. 'She was brought up in Luss, on the shore of Loch Lomond.'

'Where's that?' wondered the lad.

His father pointed over Loch Fyne to the high hills on the other side.

'If you go in that direction, you climb over a high mountain pass called Rest and be

Thankful, then you go down the other side and walk round the head of Loch Long and over a short strip of land to Loch Lomond. Your mother's home is about nine miles from there.'

'One day I'll go there,' James said. 'That would be a big adventure.'

James wasn't an especially bad boy at school; in fact, he did very well there. But despite that, he was sometimes beaten by his teacher; nearly every child was. When he knew he deserved punishment, the boy took it fair and square. But one day his teacher went too far, for he beat James so much that he broke several switches (fine wooden canes) as he did so. Whether the boy deserved any beating at all has been lost in history, but he certainly didn't deserve what he got. After school that day, he went home in a state of rebellion. Storming into the cottage, he told his mother what had happened. Normally, he didn't mention he'd been punished because his parents just punished him again, and he certainly didn't mention when his sisters were punished either. But on this occasion his father and mother realised that more punishment was not due, and they let the boy off.

'It wasn't fair,' James fumed. 'And I hate unfairness.'

'I have a letter to read to you from a missionary magazine,' said Mr Meikle, the minister, at Sunday School one day when James was thirteen years old. 'It's from a missionary in Fiji.'

The letter gripped the teenager as nothing had gripped him before. As Mr Meikle read about the difference the gospel had made in the lives of Fijian cannibals, the boy's heart raced with excitement. Having finished reading, the minister looked over his spectacles, and said, 'I wonder if there is a boy here this afternoon who will become a missionary, and who will take the good news of Jesus Christ to the cannibals.'

'I will,' James said in his heart. 'If God helps me, I'll do just that.'

Before he reached home that day, he knelt by the side of the road and asked God to make a missionary of him. When James told his parents what had happened, their hearts were moved, for they were both Christians, and they had prayed for their son since before he was born.

But there were things to do before thinking of Fiji, things like finding a job in Inveraray.

'Are you working?' a friend asked James, when they met some months after leaving school for the last time.

'Yes,' he replied. 'I've a job in the lawyer's office in Inveraray.'

'That must be interesting,' said the other lad, who was on the crew of a fishing boat.

'It's certainly an eye-opener,' commented James. He would have liked to talk about some of the things he saw and heard in the course of his work, but he thought he had better not.

'There are so many unfairnesses in life,' he thought, as he walked home that day. 'And the more I see of the legal system, I realise it's not always fair either.'

It was November 1859; it was dark, and James and some of his pals were up to no good.

'There's a revival meeting in Inveraray tonight,' one of them said, when they met. 'How about going and making just enough noise that the speaker can't be heard?'

'That sounds like fun,' sneered another.

But one of James' friends heard the plan and made another.

'I've a present for you,' he told young Chalmers, when he 'accidentally' bumped into him. 'It's a Bible. And I'm giving it to you with the suggestion that you go to the meeting tonight not to make trouble, but to hear what is said.'

That's just what James did, and he was so moved and troubled by what he heard, that the very next day he spoke to Mr Meikle, and that kindly minister led him to the Lord. From that day on, young James Chalmers was a Christian worker, and he made plans to become a missionary overseas.

It was hard work for James to train for the mission field, but Mr Meikle helped him in many ways. After long years of training and a marriage, James Chalmers and his very new wife left Scottish shores for the South Sea Islands, via Australia, on 17th October, 1865. Mrs Chalmers was hardly used to being called by that name when they left, for they had only been married two days before sailing! The voyages were not uneventful; they were threatened with shipwreck twice in the time they were at sea. Seven months and three days later, James and his wife arrived at Avarua, Rarotonga, in the South Sea Islands. They were there at last! James was immediately put to work training local men to take the gospel to the remotest parts of their homeland.

It was eleven years later that James' dream of reaching out to the cannibal people came true. That was when he and his wife moved from Rarotonga to the island of New Guinea.

'Life here will be very different,' he told his wife, on the ship. 'The people are ruled by their belief in evil spirits, and there are indescribable acts going on there. Only God can change the lives of the islanders.'

They had no sooner arrived, than the truth of what he had said was obvious.

'Those are human jawbones,' Mrs Chalmers shivered, indicating what some men were wearing as bracelets. 'And the people are painted to look so evil.'

Their new home was soon surrounded by painted men demanding knives, tomahawks and other weapons.'

'You may kill us,' James said, 'but you'll never get weapons from us.'

The next day, the ringleader returned, but this time to say he was sorry! From then on, the new missionary and his wife were shown some strange kindnesses, including being given invitations to many feasts, cannibal feasts among them.

'Is man good to eat?' Chalmers once asked an old man, who by then had become a Christian.

'Sheep and pigs are not good,' the islander replied. 'But man, he too much good.'

Sadly, Mrs Chalmers died after two years in New Guinea. And on a visit home to Scotland, James married again and took his new wife back to the country that had won his heart.

By 1882, James and his wife saw a great change in the people they worked with.

'There are no cannibal ovens here now, no feasts of human flesh and no desire for human skulls,' which was probably why he felt able to write home with an order for 'twelve dozen tomahawks, twelve dozen butcher knives' with the explanation that he was 'going east to try to make friends between the tribes.'

That may seem to be a strange way to make friends, and we can only assume that by then he knew that the weapons were being used on animals rather than humans!

'We're going back to visit Rarotonga,' James told his wife. 'I've not seen the people there since I left thirteen years ago.'

'At every house, men and women came out to join us,' Mrs Chalmers wrote home, soon after they arrived. 'The reception was wonderful! People embraced James as though they thought they'd never see him again on earth.'

It must have seemed to the pair of them that things had changed greatly for the better. No doubt they were very encouraged.

At the turn of the century, a great sadness came upon James Chalmers, when his second wife died. By way of comforting himself, the missionary kept busier than ever. Just a few months later, on 4th April, 1901, he sailed for Goaribari Island with another missionary called Oliver Tomkins, to reach out to the people there. As the boat anchored, three days later, it was swarmed with islanders.

'I promise we'll come ashore tomorrow morning,' James told them.

They kept their promise and were ashore even before they had breakfast.

'Come into the hut,' some men said, pointing to a long tribal hut not far from the shore. 'That's our feast hall.'

James and his friend accepted the invitation, as did a number of islanders who were already Christians. But the welcome that awaited them inside the hut was very different. Going from bright sunlight, the men's eyes were probably not accustomed to the dark before they were attacked. So it may be that they didn't realise what was happening. James Chalmers and Oliver Tomkins were attacked from behind and beaten with stone clubs. As they lay on the ground, they had their heads cut off. Having got rid of the missionaries, the islanders set upon the local Christians, and a terrible massacre followed. Unlike his friends on the mainland of New Guinea, the people of the Goaribari Island were still cannibals. The bodies of the murdered Christians were handed over to the women to be cooked for eating that same day.

When James Chalmers was just thirteen years old, he heard from Mr Meikle about the cannibal peoples of the world, and the thought of working among them made his heart race with excitement. There must have been some who, when they heard that he'd become a victim of cannibalism himself, thought that his life had been wasted. But

James Chalmers knew differently, although he was completely aware of the dangers. Things had changed in many parts of New Guinea, thanks to the work he did there. We know that from a letter he wrote home, not long before he died.

'These people were savages when I came to New Guinea, and a couple of years ago they were still skull hunters. Now they have the finest church in all of New Guinea and they built and paid for it themselves.'

The missionary work, however, continued in New Guinea. Men and women, natives of the islands that James had given his life for, carried on the work. It was through James that they first heard of the Lord Jesus Christ, and they knew that this work had to keep going. They mustn't give up. James had had a great sense of fairness, even as a boy at home in Inveraray. It wasn't fair that those he went to help killed him, but it was worth it to see so many become Christians.

FACT FILE

New Guinea: The easiest way to find New Guinea on the map is to find Australia and look north. New Guinea is not a single country now. The eastern part of the main island is Papua New Guinea, while the western part is part of Indonesia. The climate there is very humid, and the island is home to some remarkable animals. Among the most striking are flying foxes, which are fruit-eating bats with a wingspan of up to 1.5 metres (4.92 feet). They fly out in great swarms to roost on the branches of fruit trees around dusk.

Keynote: James prayed that God would make a missionary of him when he heard about the work with the Fijian cannibals, and his parents were very pleased. But God had to make a Christian of James before he could make a missionary of him. We need to remember that. Before we can do any great things for God, we need a right relationship with him, by putting our faith in Jesus.

Think: How do you think you would have felt if you had landed on an island and found the people with human jawbones for bracelets? Would you have found it easy to love them and to try and help them? That's what James did. Think about who you find difficult to love, and how you can make sure that you do demonstrate love for such people.

 Prayer: Lord Jesus, thank you for the people who tell me about you, even when I make it difficult for them. Teach me to love you more than anyone or any thing, and to be willing to give up anything for your sake. Amen.

Dietrich Bonhoeffer

Dietrich and his twin sister, whose name was Sabine, slipped silently from the room they were playing in, at the back of their home in Breslau, to the front of the house, where they could look out at the Catholic cemetery across the road.

'I was sure there would be a funeral this morning,' said Dietrich, who was just ten minutes older than his sister, and therefore felt that he knew significantly more than she did. 'I saw the men arriving to dig the grave.'

Sabine was silent. She knew that she could learn things from listening as well as from seeing. 'I think they're coming now,' she whispered, when she heard the slow clip-clopping of the horse-drawn hearse.

The twins watched as the horse slowed in front of their house then turned in the cemetery gate.

'The dead person must have been important,' said Sabine. 'Look how many people there are!'

Dietrich began to count, but he got in a muddle after he had reached 100, and gave up.

'There you are!' their nursery nurse said. 'I might have known the pair of you would be watching a funeral. I searched the house for you, and, when I saw the cook looking in the direction of the cemetery, I knew exactly where you would be.'

Sabine looked at the ground. She couldn't quite work out why it bothered her nurse when she and her brother watched funerals. They were the most interesting things that happened in their street, so why shouldn't they watch them?

'Come now,' the nurse insisted. 'It's time for your milk and biscuits.'

By the time the youngsters arrived for their snack, everyone else in the house had nearly finished.

'Watching another funeral, were you?' teased Karl-Friedrich. 'Was it a big one?'

'There were over a hundred people there,' Dietrich said. 'I counted.'

'But you've not started lessons with the governess yet,' Karl-Friedrich smiled. 'I don't believe that you can really count to a hundred. Why, I don't think you can even count how many people live in this house.'

'Of course I can,' pouted Dietrich. 'I'll show you.'

Dietrich began to count on his fingers, holding them steady as he did so. Everyone waited for the answer.

'It comes to seventeen,' Dietrich announced.

As his brothers and sisters looked doubtful, the lad went through them one at a time. There were his parents, three older brothers, two older sisters, Sabine, baby Suzanne, the housemaid, parlour maid, cook, governess, nursery nurse and his father's receptionist and chauffeur.'

'But that only comes to sixteen,' said the boy in a puzzled way.

Sabine knew the problem. 'You forgot to count yourself,' she told her twin.

Before they went to bed that night, Sabine and Dietrich had a discussion.

'How long are dead people dead for?' they asked Karl-Friedrich, when they couldn't decide for themselves.

'I think they're dead for eternity,' their oldest brother said. 'At least they never come back to earth again.'

When the twins went to bed, they had plenty to talk about; in fact, they always had plenty to talk about.

'What do you think being dead is like?' asked Sabine.

'It must be like having your eyes and ears shut all the time,' suggested Dietrich.

'But eternity's a long time to have your eyes and ears shut.'

'Let's try it and see,' said her twin.

Sabine and Dietrich screwed their eyes shut and tried not to listen to the sounds in the house. It was difficult, because with such a big family it was always noisy. That's how they were lying when their nursery nurse came in to tuck them up for the night.

'What are you two doing?' she asked.

Dietrich explained about their experiment.

'It's not normal for children to think so much about death,' she said, stomping about the room. 'But this family isn't quite normal. You all think far too much.'

'I can't wait to go on holiday,' Karl-Friedrich said. 'The lake will be warm enough for swimming, and we'll be able to climb and shoot and do lots of other things.'

The Bonhoeffers had a holiday home that they all loved going to. What a hustle of packing had to be done first for so many people! Although they enjoyed all their holidays there, this one was remembered for quite another reason.

'Look!' screamed Dietrich, when they were playing beside the lake.

The children looked to where he was pointing.

'It's Fräulein Lenchen!' the boy screamed again. 'She's drowning!'

Fräulein Horn, the family governess was first to move. Dashing to the side of the lake, she headed right into the water and swam to the middle. Grabbing the nursery nurse, she pulled her to the edge. Dietrich was right there beside the two women. Thumping his nurse on the back, he watched, fascinated, as Fräulein Horn pushed her fingers down her friend's throat, forcing her to cough and begin breathing again. The two women were soaking. Despite this, the governess led the children in a long 'thank you' prayer to God for saving Fräulein Lenchen's life.

The Bonhoeffers' nursery nurse must have been pleased when the family left Breslau and moved to Berlin soon afterwards; at least it would get them away from the cemetery across the road, and all the twins' talk about death. She was especially sensitive, since she nearly drowned herself. Dr Bonhoeffer's appointment as a professor at Berlin University meant they had to move to Germany's capital city.

'This is the best garden in the world!' the children decided, when they moved into their new home. 'It's huge! And there are plenty of places to have dens.'

Hours were spent outside playing games, and hours were spent inside playing music.

All the children were musical, and they often played their instruments together.

'We can't all play at once,' Suzanne said, when she was just old enough to join in.

'Why not?' asked one of her brothers.

Suzanne giggled. 'If we all play, that leaves nobody to be the audience!'

There was much fun and laughter in the Bonhoeffer household. They were a happy crew, although things around them in Germany were not always as happy as they were. And by 1914, when Dietrich and Sabine were eight years old, they found themselves living in a country at war, a war that lasted for four long years.

'Does Walter have to join the army as well as Karl-Friedrich?' Sabine asked. The idea seemed scary to her.

'We should be proud that they're both soldiers for the Fatherland,' said Professor Bonhoeffer.

The night before Walter enlisted, Dietrich wrote words to a popular song and sang them to his brother. 'Now at last, we say Godspeed on your journey,' was the opening line.

The First World War marked the end of the Bonhoeffers' happy home. Both Karl-Friedrich and Walter were wounded. Although the older boy recovered from his wounds, Walter did not. He died during an operation to save his life. And it was as though something died inside Mrs Bonhoeffer. From a lively and happy mother, she slipped into a deep depression that affected her whole family. Even though her husband, who was a psychiatrist, did everything he could to support and help her, it was a long time before she was anything like her former self again.

When Dietrich was in his mid-teens, his schoolteacher asked each person in the class what they wanted to do when they grew up.

'You are all very clever,' said Herr Klein-Schmidt, 'so much so that you'll be able to choose from many careers.'

'I want to be a doctor,' said one boy.

Another had decided to be a chemist, and a third told the class he hoped to be a general in the army.

'And you, Bonhoeffer?' said Herr Klein-Schmidt. 'What are you going to do with your life?'

'I want to be a theologian,' said Dietrich.

There was a silence in the classroom as everyone considered their friend's reply.

'I want to study all about God, and all that everyone thinks about God,' explained Dietrich.

'You mean you want to be a minister,' said his teacher, who was half-German and half-Jewish.

'No,' the teenager replied. 'I don't want to be a minister. I want to be a theologian.'

Dietrich's decision produced much the same effect at home. Professor Bonhoeffer had hoped that his sons would study science or medicine, but he respected Dietrich's decision, even if he was more than a little puzzled by it.

Walter's death was the first real shock in Dietrich's life. The second happened just after he started university in 1923.

'My name's Rolf Hoftstag,' a fellow student said. 'And you're Bonhoeffer.'

Dietrich agreed that was who he was.

'I wondered if you'd like to come to join the Hedgehogs,' said Rolf. 'I understand that your father used to be a member.'

He wasn't sure what to do, but because Rolf made no effort to move away, Dietrich agreed to join. The meetings he went to seemed harmless enough, if a little boring.

'Are you a Hedgehog?' Dietrich asked another student he met.

'No,' the young man said awkwardly. 'My name's Sol Friesberg.'

Bonhoeffer was really puzzled. It was as though by telling his name, Sol assumed his friend would know why he wasn't a Hedgehog. Seeing his puzzlement, Sol Friesberg explained that Hedgehogs hated Jewish people, that they were an anti-Semitic organisation. (Anti-Semitism means hatred of Jewish people.) Dietrich was horrified, but he soon discovered that what Sol told him was quite true.

The Hedgehogs were not the only ones in Germany, at that time, that hated Jewish people. Just as Dietrich was discovering about personal faith in Jesus, and as he was committing himself to a life of serving the Lord as a theologian, so others were committing themselves to a life of service to the Fatherland. By the early 1930s, racism, especially anti-Semitism, was sweeping through Germany, and it often erupted into violence. In 1932, the Nazis won 32 per cent of the seats in parliament. Dietrich recognised what was happening and tried to encourage his fellow German Christians to stand up against the state but, in the main, church leaders didn't see what was happening before their very eyes. Some even supported the Nazi cause.

The following year, Adolf Hitler became Reich Chancellor, and the stage began to be set for World War Two. What horrified Dietrich was not the prospect of war with other countries, but what he recognised as a war between the various people of Germany, especially the war that began to be waged against the Jewish people. And when he thought back to his schooldays, and remembered the kindly half-German, half-Jewish, Herr Klein-Schmidt, the thought made him so sad he could have wept.

'I hear that Dietrich Bonhoeffer has been arrested,' a church leader said to his friend in the spring of 1943. 'Is that true?'

'I'm afraid it is,' was the reply. 'He certainly knows how to rub Adolf Hitler up the wrong way.'

'What do you mean?'

'It doesn't help with Bonhoeffer being a leader in the anti-Nazi Confessing Church. Hitler was certainly not impressed when Bonhoeffer took part in the Abwehr resistance circle.'

'Speak more quietly,' the church leader whispered. 'If we're overheard, we could both end up in prison with Bonhoeffer.'

'But I think one of the final straws was when Dietrich tried to help a group of Jewish people escape to Switzerland,' his friend said very quietly.

'You would think Bonhoeffer would realise the only way we can do any good in Germany just now, is to appear to support Hitler. If we don't, we'll be dead, and we won't do any good that way.'

The other man shook his head sadly. 'I'm not so sure,' he said. 'Sometimes I think that the world twenty years from now will think we've done nothing and condemn us. People won't know that we've tried to influence German politics from behind the scenes.'

'Shut your mouth, man!' whispered his companion urgently. 'If you're overheard, you'll be shot!'

'I'll say just one last thing, then I'm going.'

'What's that?'

'I think that Dietrich Bonhoeffer may be right. I think that even from prison, he's an inspiration to people who have more courage than I have. I wish I was as brave a man as he is.'

With that he turned on his heels and walked away, his head bent down and his shoulders drooped in depression.

Although Dietrich Bonhoeffer was in prison, and in solitary confinement, he was not idle, at least not as long as he had a pen in his hand. Letters, thoughts and articles were written, though not all found their way out of prison.

'You must remember to read and memorise Scripture,' he wrote to a friend. 'It will maintain your strength better than anything else ... Be sure to pray for all of us here. Some of these men are miserable to the point of death.'

Death was on Dietrich's mind in prison, as it had been when he stood as a child watching funerals. But now he could not count how many went to funerals. 'How many millions have died?' he asked himself, as he thought about the war. 'And how many Jewish people have perished?'

Closing his eyes, he thought of eternity.

On 9th April, 1945, Dietrich was taken from his cell and hanged in Flossenburg. His crime was his participation in the small Protestant resistance movement. Not every Christian would agree with what Bonhoeffer did, or with some of his politically motivated activities, but none can doubt that he died a Christian man, and a martyr to the Christian faith. His theology, for he was a theologian, still influences Christian thinking, especially in some parts of Europe.

FACT FILE

The Nazis: After its defeat in the First World War, Germany became a very poor country, where there was a great deal of unemployment and discontent. The leader of the National Socialist Party (or Nazis, as they were called) was actually an Austrian: Adolf Hitler. He thought that Austria and Germany should be one country, that the Jews were to blame for Germany's loss in the First World War, and that the Jewish culture and race were inferior to that of the German people. Many were attracted to this because it gave them someone to blame, and, when the Nazis came to power in 1933, this led to the Holocaust, in which over 6 million Jewish people were killed.

Keynote: When Dietrich joined the Hedgehogs, he did not realise what their aims were, but it did not take him long to find out. We must be very careful about the organisations that we join and the people that we allow to influence us. Many people find it more difficult to leave such organisations, than Dietrich did. Sometimes we may even have to tell our friends that what they are doing is wrong, and that we cannot go along with it.

Think: Many people in Germany thought that they should keep quiet about what the Nazis were doing, in order to avoid persecution, and that they could work quietly behind the scenes to oppose Hitler. In the end, however, the two men discussing Bonhoeffer were proved right. History did condemn those who kept quiet, and Hitler turned on many of them. Think about how you can stand up for those who are being picked on and can't stand up for themselves.

Pray: Lord Jesus, please stop anything like the Holocaust ever happening again. Please give me the courage to stand up for those whom others ignore and pick on. Thank you for showing us how to care for those for whom no one else cares. Amen.

Nate Saint

Rachel looked out of the window and smiled. It had been raining, but the rain clouds were blowing towards the west, and a watery sun had begun to shine.

'It's ideal for fishing,' she told her little brother. 'Does that appeal to you?'

Nate was off like an arrow from a bow.

'I'll go dig worms!' he said, as he slammed the kitchen door behind him.

Fourteen-year-old Rachel smiled. If there was something that always brought a smile to her brother's face, it was the thought of fishing in the creek. Sitting down by the window to read until Nate was ready, she picked up her favourite book, bar none. *Fifty Missionary Stories Every Child Should Know* was just right for any time of day.

'If I've got ages, I can read right through the book,' she told her father. 'And if I only have half-an-hour, I can read one story.'

Mr Saint laughed. 'If you only have two minutes, you can read just a paragraph, because you know what comes before it and happens after it. In fact, I think you could probably close the book and tell me all the stories in it off by heart.'

Before Rachel could show if that was true or not, Nate appeared in the door. His knees were muddy, his eyes shone like stars, and he was in the process of preventing a worm making a bid for freedom over the top of his bait can.

'In you go,' he said. 'And stay there!'

'There might be nine years between Rachel and Nate,' thought Mr Saint, as he watched them head off in the direction of the creek, 'but they get on really well together.'

It was September 1928, and five-year-old Nate was as happy as could be. With a fishing rod over his shoulder, a can of worms dangling from his hand, his big sister at his side, and the thought of an afternoon fishing in the creek, the lad grinned in total satisfaction. If anyone had suggested to the boy that there was anywhere in the world better than Huntingdon Valley, north of Philadelphia, he would have argued the toss!

Two years later, Nate's grin was so big it almost reached from ear to ear, thanks to his brother Sam.

'Do you want to come with me for a flight in a plane?' the older boy asked.

Did he! Hardly big enough to see over the edge of the open cockpit, Nate imagined what he couldn't actually see and thought it was the best day of his life so far. Two years later, Sam let Nate sit side by side with him at the controls of a larger cabin plane.

'Want to take her over for a minute or two?' the older lad asked.

With eyes wide in excitement, and mouth open in concentration, Nate took over the controls. Tugging the wheel gently, he felt the aircraft respond. It was as though he and the plane were one.

'Nate's eleven years old,' Mr Saint wrote to a friend, 'and his main interest is in aviation.'

How right he was. If his son wasn't dreaming about flying, he was talking about it or reading about it! Not only that, he built a six-foot long glider from a drawing he found in a magazine.

'Anyone coming to help me fly her?' he asked, when the glider was finished.

There were times when it was useful being one of a family of seven boys and one girl. It meant there was always someone willing to lend a hand with the latest madcap adventure.

'I'll come,' one of his brothers volunteered, and the pair set off with the glider and flew it like a kite at the local school's athletic field.

Two years later, in the summer of 1936, Nate went to a Christian camp in the Poconos. Having been brought up in a Christian home, the teenager knew that he had to believe in the Lord Jesus for himself, and that he had to tell others about his faith. On a Saturday night, that he would remember for the rest of his life, he told the other campers that he was a Christian. Later that same year, he spoke at a young people's meeting in his own church about what it meant to him to be a Christian. Within a few months, Nate discovered that being a Christian didn't exempt him from problems. He developed a serious bone condition called osteomyelitis that kept him in bed for months.

Europe was at war. America had joined in, and Nate was just the right age for service. Not only that, he already held his Private Pilot's Ticket. Much to his delight he was eventually accepted for the Air Cadet Training Program.

'You ought to see the outfit we get!' he wrote home. 'Complete fleece-lined flying suit and helmet, fleece-lined leather flying boots coated with waterproof vulcanised rubber, plain leather helmet and a beautiful leather jacket and gloves.'

Just as he thought he was heading for the skies, his old medical trouble flared up again, and he was declared unfit for flying.

'I turned twenty yesterday,' Nate told a friend. 'It was a kind of rough birthday present to be told that, instead of going to the airport for my first day of flying, I was going to the base for an X-ray.'

Several weeks in hospital followed, before the young cadet was on his feet again. But there was more to being in the Air Cadet Training Program than flying planes, as Nate was to find out.

'What did you do today?' his friend asked, as they relaxed one evening.

Grinning, Nate replied, 'I took a Tommy gun apart, studied it, and put it together again ... with my eyes closed!'

What the young man didn't know, was that God needed Nate to be a good mechanic, and there was no better training than the Air Cadet Training Program. Though it wasn't always easy to understand why things worked out as they did, Nate Saint knew God makes no mistakes. The picture began to come together when God called Nate to be a missionary. Thinking about it, the young man realised that his flying experience and his knowledge of mechanics went hand in hand. After all, he thought, I might need mechanical help in the back of beyond.

'Dear Nate,' wrote Mr Saint. 'I think you'll find the enclosed article interesting.'

The young man unfolded the magazine and read, 'On Wings of the Wind.' Sitting down, he read on and discovered that it was about the Christian Airmen's Missionary Fellowship, a group of airmen who served missionaries working in remote areas.

'What do I have to offer a group like that?' he asked himself.

And the answer was staring him in the face – he had his Private Pilot's Ticket and a Mechanic's Licence!

'I'll write to the Christian Airmen's Missionary Fellowship,' decided Nate.

And that's just what he did. (The Christian Airmen's Missionary Fellowship became Missionary Aviation Fellowship in 1946.)

'I want to further the cause of Christ in any way I can,' he explained in his letter, 'so count me in and keep me informed of the goings-on.'

Having signed the letter, Nate sat back in his chair and thought about the future.

So it was that having completed his time in the Air Cadet Training Program in 1946, Nate enrolled for Bible School, then dropped out because the Christian Airmen's Missionary Fellowship asked him to come on board right away. There was work to be done in Mexico, and he was the man to do it. But the work for which Nate Saint is best remembered was done in Ecuador. He went there in September 1948 when he was twenty-five years old, and he did not go alone, because he and Marj (Marjory Farris) had been married on Valentine's Day that year. Before leaving for Ecuador, Nate spoke about mission work on the radio.

'During the last war,' he said, 'we saw big bombers on the assembly line, yet we knew that of those bombers many would not accomplish even five missions over enemy territory. We also knew that young fellows ... would ride in those airborne machine-gun turrets, and their life expectancy behind those guns was, with the trigger down, only four minutes. Tremendous expendability! Missionaries constantly face expendability, and people who do not know the Lord ask why in the world we waste our lives. ... Those who have gone to tribes who have never heard the gospel gladly count themselves expendable. And they count it all joy.'

'What's it like flying in Ecuador?' a friend wrote, after the Saints had been there for some months.

'It has its moments,' Nate thought, remembering some of the hair-raising situations the difficult terrain produced. It didn't take him long to decide which one to describe.

'I was flying over Quito just three months after we arrived here. There were two passengers, a mother and her son. Take-off was perfect, but within minutes I knew there was trouble. A strong gust of wind roared over the mountains and slammed into the plane, forcing it downwards. I did my best to control the plane, but it crashed into the ground below. My passengers weren't badly injured, but I spent a month in hospital and another five months in a body cast. Jungle flying can be dangerous,' he concluded, 'but it is what God has called me to do.'

The Saints were not the only missionaries working in Ecuador with the Quetchua people, and Nate often found himself helping Ed McCully, Jim Elliot and Peter Fleming and their wives with their work. In 1955 these young missionaries became convinced that God wanted them to reach out to the Huaorani people, and to tell them about the Lord Jesus. They seemed to hold the same conversation over and over again.

'They are the most dangerous people I've ever heard of.'

'Their name in the local language is Auca, and that means savage.'

'They've killed people who've gone into their villages.'

'They are the fiercest people in Ecuador.'

'Which is why they need to hear about Jesus.'

The young men, their wives, and their children (by then the Saints had two sons and a daughter) prayed about it and felt sure that God wanted them to share the good news with these terrifying people.

In September 1955, Nate and Ed found a Huaorani settlement fifteen minutes by air from their mission station. It was time to make firm plans.

'We won't tell anyone but our wives,' said Jim, when the young men discussed it. 'Otherwise the press and adventurers will try to join us.'

'We'll have to learn some Huaorani from Dayuma.'

Nate smiled, thankful that his sister Rachel had rescued Dayuma after her Huaorani husband was killed.

'I think we should fly over the village regularly,' suggested Nate, 'and lower gifts to the people to show them that we're friendly.'

Nate's inventiveness produced a means of lowering gifts. He discovered that if he lowered a bucket from the plane then flew in tight circles, the bucket remained still enough for one of the Huaorani people to take something out of it. Week after week they circled the village, taking presents with them each time. Soon the Huaorani men responded with gifts by return: a woven headband, carved combs, two live parrots, parcels of peanuts, even a piece of smoked monkey tail!

'We've been in contact with the villagers for three months now,' the young missionary couples decided. 'Now we've got to make contact face to face.'

'We need a fifth man for that,' someone suggested. 'And I think that Roger Youderian is our man.'

A former Paratrooper, Roger was working as a missionary with the Jivaros people, and he was quite at home in the jungle.

'I think we could land on that river beach,' Nate said, when the five young men were making their final plans. 'It's just four miles from the village.'

'Do we take guns?' Ed asked.

'I think we should,' said Peter. 'We could fire them into the air to ward off an attack if necessary. But we'll not use them as weapons, even to save our lives. Agreed?'

'Agreed,' the other four said together.

Having prayed with their wives and families, the missionaries agreed on radio contact details before Nate, Ed, Jim, Peter and Roger climbed aboard the Missionary Aviation Fellowship aircraft for the biggest adventure of their lives. It was Tuesday. They flew in, set up camp, then circled over the village. On Friday a Huaorani man, woman and teenaged girl arrived, stayed a few hours, then left.

'This IS the day,' Nate radioed early on Sunday afternoon, 8th January, 1956. 'I can see ten men coming. It looks like they'll be here for an afternoon service!'

Nate, Ed, Jim, Peter and Roger went to the Huaorani people with the good news that Jesus Christ is the one and only Saviour. The Huaorani men who met them that day at the river arrived with murderous spears. When the five young missionaries didn't contact their wives at 4.30 pm as arranged, the women knew there was something wrong. Their husbands set out on a great adventure, but their greatest adventure of all was in meeting the Lord Jesus when they went home to heaven, killed by the people they went to help.

Less than three years later Rachel Saint (Nate's sister) and Elisabeth Elliott (Jim's wife) were back among the Huaorani people. Today there is a Huaorani church and Bible training college. During the construction of the college, Missionary Aviation Fellowship helped airlift in the building materials. When Nate and Marj's children, Kathy and Stephen, wanted to be baptised, it was two of those who had killed Nate and his four companions who baptised them.

FACT FILE

Access by air: Many of the places that Nate and his colleagues flew to in Ecuador and around the world were totally inaccessible by either road or sea. Before 1900, nobody could access these places because there were no aeroplanes, but after planes had been invented, these inaccessible areas were opened up. The first powered flight was made by Wilbur Wright on 17 December, 1903, but it only flew 9.7 metres (31.8 feet) off the ground. Nate had to climb a lot higher than that to get over the Andes mountains when he was flying in Ecuador.

Keynote: Nate was willing to count himself expendable for the sake of taking the gospel to people in Mexico and South America. He did this because he could see himself as part of a larger plan to reach out to these people. Although he died before that was fulfilled, his sister saw fruit from his labours. God's purposes are always fulfilled in the end.

Think: Nate was disappointed not to be able to go flying in the Air Cadet Training Program, but the mechanical skills he learned during that period proved very useful in later life. He realised that God never makes any mistakes, and that he has a purpose in every experience, although we might not understand it. God is still the same God, and we need to learn to trust him and to seek to serve him, even when we find ourselves in places that we would rather not be.

 Prayer: Lord Jesus, it is good to know that you never make mistakes and that you are in control of everything. Please help me to trust you and to follow you in everything that I do, even when it is difficult to understand what is going on. Amen.

Ivan Moiseyev

The snow fell, more snow landing on more snow landing on yet more snow. Only the bright whiteness of the snow made the day seem bearable. Everything else was dull and drab, like a picture with all the bright colours washed out. And it was so very cold.

Vanya (that was Ivan's pet name) stood at the window of his home looking out. He had a choice to make, but he didn't know which of the three alternatives to choose. He could take off his thick gloves and rub his hands together at the risk of them ending up colder than they were with his gloves on, or he could take his gloves off and heat his hands at the little stove and maybe get chilblains again this year, or he could warm his gloves at the stove and hope that the heat would penetrate through to his fingertips. Remembering the terrible pain of last winter's chilblains, he decided on the third option. Keeping his gloves on, he warmed them by the stove and sighed with relief when feeling surged back into his fingers. Then what he knew would happen did happen. It was as though the warmth set his fingers on fire. Oh, the pain of it! Eleven-year-old Vanya tucked his hands under his arms, clapped them together, waved them in the air ... anything to hurry on the process of comfort coming back. Then, as suddenly as the pain began, it was over. Grinning at his mother who had watched the whole performance, Vanya removed his gloves and took a piece of black bread and cheese from the table.

'That's good,' he said, losing some breadcrumbs as he spoke. 'The cold makes me hungry.'

'Why are the winters so cold and so long in Volontirovka?' Vanya asked his mother, who was nursing the baby of the family.

She smiled at her good-looking son. 'That is how God made them,' she said.

'If I made the weather, I'd make freezing winters short and the summers long and hot.'

His mother got up to put the baby to bed. As she passed the window, she glanced outside.

'Come and see this,' she said softly.

Vanya went to the window and looked out. The snow had stopped falling, and pale sunlight was turning the whiteness of the newly fallen snow into shimmering silver.

'What God made is very beautiful,' the woman said.

Vanya's eyes shone like the snow and he had to agree.

Taking another piece of black bread, and sitting down by the stove to enjoy it, the lad watched as his mother wrapped the baby in a shawl, then laid him on a ledge near the stove. Vanya smiled as he thought of the family's sleeping arrangements. At night the two youngest were wrapped tight, then put near the stove where they would benefit from the little heat that was left in it. Then the older children slept on couches and cots wherever there was room in the little house.

'I think we have the coldest of all corners,' Semyon often complained to Vanya.

'Maybe we do,' his brother always replied. 'But the little ones need more heat than we do.'

The cold often kept Semyon and Vanya awake, and they whispered in the darkness to each other.

'What do you want to do when you grow up?' Vanya asked his brother.

Semyon thought of the collective farm on which they lived, a farm that belonged to the state and on which most of the people in the village of Volontirovka worked.

'Well I'm not going to spend my life working my fingers to the bone on the farm, that's for certain,' the boy said. 'I'll make sure I know the right people, then get a job organising the collective farms. Sitting at a desk must be better than slaving in the mud or trying to hack your way through packed ice to dig up winter vegetables.'

Vanya listened to the bitterness in his brother's voice.

'That's why I work hard in Young Pioneers,' went on Semyon. 'The more people who get to know me the better. That's what matters in Moldavia.'

'It's time you boys were going to sleep,' their father said through the darkness. 'Goodnight.'

'Goodnight, Papa,' both lads replied at once. Then they turned round, snuggled their backs against each other for warmth, and dreamed their own dreams.

'Home first again!' Vanya's mother said, as he ran in the door. 'There's bread and cold fish on the table.'

Licking his lips at the thought of the fish, the boy said, 'Mama, there's something I need to ask you.'

Lifting the baby to burp him, the woman waited for what was to come.

'Why does my teacher say that there is no god? He says that people who believe in a god are like men who can't walk and who need crutches to lean on. Are you and Papa like men who can't walk? That's what Semyon says.'

The woman shook her head sadly. Semyon caused his Christian parents a great deal of heartache. He seemed to be taking in all that he was taught by his teachers and at Young Pioneers. It worried her that he would one day become a real Communist, and forget all he'd learned at home about the Lord Jesus Christ being the one and only Saviour.

'It's the other way round,' Vanya's mother said. 'Because Communists don't believe in God, they need Communism to tell them what to do and what to think. Although they can't see it for themselves, they are using Communism as a crutch.'

'Is that what Semyon's doing?' the boy asked.

His mother didn't reply, partly because the baby had just brought up some milk on her shawl, and partly because she was praying for Semyon.

In Vanya's teenage years he asked the questions that all teenagers ask. He wanted to know the whys, hows, wheres, and whats of life. That was how he discovered about Communism from his parents; and what he learned from them was different from his school history lessons. It saddened him that, after the Russian Revolution in 1917, his country should have turned its back on Christianity and tried to build a society that excluded God. And by the time he was sixteen years old, Vanya realised that not only could God not be excluded from the world he had made, Vanya could not exclude the Lord from his heart. Vanya felt God's call to believe in him, and he came to a saving faith in Jesus. That was in 1968, and within a short time of becoming a Christian, he was speaking in church about his faith.

'You'll get yourself into trouble with the authorities,' his friends told him. 'If they discover that you're becoming a preacher, you might find yourself in Siberia working in a mine for more years than you want to think about.'

'The Bible tells us to spread the good news about the Lord Jesus to those who don't know him,' Vanya replied. 'So do I obey God or the Communists?'

'You obey your god if you like,' one of the young men said. 'But don't speak to me again when we meet in the street, because I don't want to end up in Siberia just for being a friend of Ivan Moiseyev.'

Even Semyon, who didn't agree with what Vanya believed, warned his brother to be careful, or he'd get himself into trouble. 'The Baptists are not a recognised organisation,' he said, 'so that makes going to their services illegal.'

Although Vanya knew that Communists only tolerated Christians if they kept quiet about what they believed, he was both unable and unwilling to do that. God had saved his soul, and he was determined to tell others that he could save them too.

Having trained as a taxi driver after leaving school, when Vanya was eighteen years old, he joined the Red Army for his compulsory two years of national service. So from working as a civilian taxi driver he changed to serving as an army chauffeur, not an easy job in Odessa, where the snow had already started for the winter. Vanya's first priority when he moved into barracks was to find a quiet place where he could pray each day. He had to leave his Christian friends at home, but God went with him into the Red Army. It wasn't long before he came up against the army authorities, and it was because he prayed so long one morning that he was late for drill.

'You were late because you were praying!' said the astounded officer. 'There'll be no more of that!'

The result was that Vanya was reported to the Polit-Ruk where he was 'reminded' that the Communists had proved scientifically that God didn't exist. Instead of keeping his mouth shut, the young soldier told the official from the Polit-Ruk what the Bible had to say about the existence of God.

'You need to learn a lesson,' the man said. 'As you seem to like being on your knees, you can get down on your knees and scrub the drill hall and all the corridors in the barracks. That will take you all night. And while you are on your knees scrubbing, you can think about Communist teaching.'

From that day on Vanya was a marked man, and a very close watch was kept on what he did, and to whom he spoke.

It was 1971, and it was cold, very cold. Dreadful news had spread around the barracks about Vanya, and those who knew him couldn't wait to get the story straight.

'What happened to you?' a friend asked him, when they met shortly afterwards.

'Just another punishment for speaking about the Lord,' Vanya shrugged.

'Tell me about it.'

Vanya sighed. 'Corporal Gidenko decided to "bring me to my senses" once and for all. So he ordered me to stand outside all night until I was ready to apologise for talking about my faith.'

'Outside! But it's more than 13 degrees below zero at night,' his friend responded.

'And he made me wear just a cotton summer uniform,' Vanya said. 'The cold was terrible, and I thought I'd freeze to death. But I prayed to God and was warmed.'

'That must have been the longest night of your life,' his comrade said.

Vanya looked at him. 'But it was twelve nights. I stood outside in sub-zero temperatures in my light summer uniform for twelve nights.'

'Are you superhuman?' asked his amazed friend.

'No,' said Vanya. 'I'm just an ordinary human being who believes in Almighty God.'

Soon after that terrible punishment, God spoke to Vanya in a dream, a dream in which he saw and spoke to an angel. Being the young man he was, Vanya shared his dream with anyone who would listen to him. His commanding officers were nearly tearing their hair out!

'If making him stand outside for twelve nights at this time of year doesn't stop him speaking about his god, I really don't know what will,' said one officer.

'That punishment made him worse than ever,' added another. 'It seems that his god sent an angel to comfort him – and he's telling the whole barracks about it!' Then, as an afterthought, the man added, 'Nobody believes it, of course. All the soldiers know it's rubbish.'

But that wasn't the case at all. There were those who through Vanya discovered the reality of God for themselves.

'Don't tell our parents everything,' Vanya wrote to his brother Vladimir on 15th July, 1972. 'Just tell them that Vanya wrote you a letter, and he says that Jesus Christ is going into battle. Tell them that it's a Christian battle, and Vanya doesn't know whether he'll be back.' Vladimir read on to the end of the letter with a lump in his throat. 'Remember this one verse,' Vanya wrote, before signing his name, 'Be faithful unto death, and I will give you the crown of life.'

The following day twenty-year-old Vanya was dead. And having been faithful to the point of death, God did give him the crown of life.

His body was returned to his parents' home for burial. Although they were told that Vanya had drowned, his father and mother wished to see his body. The army officers who accompanied the coffin left before they could do that, perhaps because they had seen the marks of Vanya's last punishments. He had been tortured for his faith before being killed by drowning. It was July when the young man was buried. There was no snow on the ground, and his home village looked at its summer best. Many gathered round to support Vanya's family, some carrying garland Bible texts in the Moldavian and Russian languages.

Soon afterwards, a letter arrived from four Red Army soldiers who had served with Vanya. 'Dear Moiseyev family,' they wrote. 'Don't be discouraged. God has done a great work in the salvation of souls through your dear son and our brother and friend. ... Let them punish us, deprive us of everything on this earth, but they will not be able to take the freedom of Christ out of our hearts.'

Vanya had died and gone to heaven, but God still had his brave Christian soldiers in Russia's Red Army.

FACT FILE

Communist Russia: The Communist Party came to power in Russia in November 1917, after a popular uprising against the increasingly unpopular Tsar and a second uprising against a less extreme government, which was unable to provide the reforms demanded by many Russians. The Communist Party established a one party state in Russia and nationalised land and many of the industries. This often had disastrous consequences. No dissent, either religious or political, was allowed, and many people who spoke against the government were sent to prison camps, known as Gulags, in Siberia.

Keynote: Vanya found that the Communists were telling him to do one thing, while God, through the Bible, was telling him to do another. He chose to tell people about Jesus, even when it meant that he would be subject to very cruel punishments. It is not always easy to tell people about Jesus, but he has given us the responsibility, and he will give us strength and encouragement to do it, just as he did for Vanya.

Think: Although Vanya was far from Christian friends and his parents when he was sent to serve in the Red Army, God was still with him, and he was still able to pray, whatever the Polit-Ruk had to say. They could not stop him by their arguments, any more than the Communists could prove that God did not exist with science. Wherever you are, you can still pray to God and be confident that he will help you.

 Prayer: Lord Jesus, thank you for all that you have done for me and for remaining faithful wherever I am. Please give me the strength not to deny you, even when others try to make me do so. Amen.

Graham Staines

The sun was shining brightly on the Sunshine Coast in Queensland, Australia. From Double Island Point in the north, to the Glass House Mountains in the south, the blue sky was unbroken by a single cloud. As young people awoke that morning, they first checked the piles of Christmas presents at the ends of their beds, then they ran to their windows to see whether they'd be having their Christmas dinner on the beach, by the barbecue or (dreadful thought) in their homes. When Graham looked out on Palmwoods, there was no doubt in his mind that by early afternoon the barbecue would be glowing red, and delicious smells would fill the air. Meanwhile, there were things to do ... and most of them were wrapped in brightly coloured Christmas paper! One parcel after another was opened, and each seemed to be more exciting than the one that went before. But there was something he was especially looking for;

after all, he'd dropped enough hints. It was almost with a sense of relief that he noticed the book-shaped parcel right at the bottom. Graham smiled. 'That's it,' he said, as he unwrapped the book carefully. It wouldn't have been every teenager's choice of books, but *The Flora and Fauna of Queensland* was exactly what Graham Staines wanted. As he flicked through the pages, flowers and insects, trees and animals flashed past him. He could hardly wait till evening. The boy grinned. 'Don't be stupid!' he thought. 'It's Christmas, and there's a lot to enjoy before evening.'

Dinner was round the barbecue, and what a meal to celebrate with. By the end of it, Graham was lying on a lounger dressed in a pair of shorts that were a bit tighter than usual, thanks to what he had just eaten.

'Those barbecued buttered pineapple slices were delicious,' he said. 'But I'm stuffed!'

Although his mind wanted to play some of the games he'd been given for Christmas, all his eyes wanted to do were close. And that's what happened. Minutes later, Graham and the other members of his family were snoozing happily. Strangely, it was the buttered pineapple slices that inspired the boy's dream. He was no sooner asleep than he imagined himself walking through the tropical fruit plantations for which Palmwoods was famous. He pictured vast hands of bananas growing upwards, looking far too heavy to stay on the tree. His dream was so vivid he could smell warm peachiness, he could feel the cosy velvet-covered apricots ... and of course there were pineapples, great big, juicy pineapples. The smell of them seemed to be everywhere. Suddenly wide awake, Graham realised that they were not a dream; more buttered pineapple slices were on the barbecue. Delicious!

Hours later, back in his room with *The Flora and Fauna of Queensland* propped open on the table and a blank airmail letter in front of him, Graham thought how different Christmas would have been for his friend Shantanu Satpathy.

'I guess Baripada in India will have been as hot today as it is in Palmwoods, Australia, but I don't think Shantanu will have had buttered pineapple.'

But the thought of Shantanu sent Graham to his book and his sketch pad. A few days previously he had found a brightly coloured beetle that he'd never seen before. Rather than capture the creature, he drew a detailed picture of it. And he had just looked it up in his new book and wanted to write and tell his Indian pen-friend about it.

'I'd love to see the insects Shantanu tells me about,' he thought. 'I wonder if I will ever go to India, or if that's just a dream.'

Graham laughed aloud.

'My dream about the pineapple slices turned out to be true, so maybe one day I'll go to India after all.'

Having written a long and detailed letter to Shantanu, fifteen-year-old Graham lay on top of his bed and thought teenaged thoughts. And the particular thought that wouldn't go away was a real contradiction to his day. It was Christmas. He'd had a happy day with plenty of gifts that showed he was wanted and loved. Not only that, he'd wandered around the garden in his shorts knowing that he looked bronzed and healthy. So why did the picture he'd seen of Josia Soren keep coming into his mind? Why would the sight of a Mayurbhanj boy with leprosy not go away when he opened his eyes? Why could he see the patches on the lad's skin, his damaged nose and his missing fingertips, whether his eyes were open or shut? Why did the sight of a leprous boy his own age affect him in a way that nothing in his life had ever affected him before?

Lying there on top of his bed, Graham Staines knew what it was to be a boy and to be almost grown up at the same time. The boy in him wanted to weep at the sight of Josia Soren, while the almost man in him made plans about what he could do.

'There must be some treatment for leprosy, if only it could reach those who need it,' he thought. 'And boys like Josia could be trained to do work so that they wouldn't be so poor.' Before he fell asleep, Graham had made all sorts of plans for what could be done for the likes of Josia Soren. But when he finally nodded off to sleep, it was the smell of buttered pineapple on the barbecue that wafted into his dreams.

Nine years later, and after many letters to and from Shantanu Satpathy, Graham sat on top of the same bed in the same room wondering if he was dreaming.

'Am I really leaving for India in a few hours?' he asked himself.

In fact, he almost nipped his arm to check he was awake. India had been his dream for so long it seemed almost impossible that it was now about to become a reality. But it was. The following day, that's where he was! A tingle went from the soles of his feet to the hair on his head when he touched Indian soil for the very first time.

'This is like coming home,' he thought, then his mind immediately turned to his pen-friend.

Graham laughed. 'And in no time at all I'll meet Shantanu! We've written to each other about all sorts of things, especially the plants and animals of India and Australia.

But I wonder what we'll talk about when we meet face to face. I can't imagine that he'll suddenly go on about Asian elephants, and I'll respond with a discourse on the kangaroo!'

Of course it wasn't like that at all, and the pen-friends were soon firm friends who had no problem finding things to talk about.

Although years had passed since Graham first saw Josia Soren's photo, it was one of the biggest influences in all of his life. Graham had become a Christian while still young, and God had used Josia to put a calling into his heart, a calling to help those afflicted by leprosy. Where better to do that than in India where the disease was a scourge that blighted many lives? So, having at last reached India in 1965, Graham Staines just remained there. He joined the staff of the Evangelical Missionary Society of Mayurbhanj in Rairangpur.

'What do I write here?' Graham asked himself, as he filled out an application form for the work permit that would allow him to remain in India. 'I know. I'll say that I'm involved in missionary work, and that I also work with the Mayurbhanj Leprosy Home and Rajabasa Leprosy Rehabilitation Farm.'

Having decided on the words, he had to use small writing to squeeze them into the space provided. In another part of the form,

Graham explained that he 'preached the gospel as and when time permitted.'

Reading through the rest of the application, he came on a request for his 'profession or present occupation'. That caused him some head-scratching, as he'd already put the work he was doing. Thinking through what he was able to do, he picked up the pen again and wrote, 'I'm a missionary trained in carpentry, metalwork and motor mechanics, and a clerk trained in accountancy.'

With all those skills, Graham Staines was a useful person to have around!

'Do you speak the language?' a visitor to Rairangpur asked Graham, after the Australian had been working there for some time.

'What language would that be?' the missionary smiled.

'Em ... whatever they speak here.'

'Well, the people here speak a variety of languages, because they come from a variety of places. But I suppose you could say I speak the language because I've learned Oriya, Santhali and Ho.'

'You must have spent years at university!' was the amazed reply.

Collecting the tools he needed to help a disabled leprosy patient, Graham smiled. 'Yes,' he said. 'I've been at the University of Life.' Seeing the puzzlement in the visitor's face, he explained, 'I've learned the languages by spending time with people who speak them.'

In 1983 Graham met Gladys, the young woman who was to become his wife. She was also Australian, having been brought up just over twenty miles from Palmwoods! But God took them both to India and had them meet each other there. Gladys was a Christian who had already served the Lord in Singapore, Malaysia, Europe, Australia and India. The year they married, the couple moved to another Evangelical Missionary Society of Mayurbhanj Leprosy Home, this one at Baripada. Graham took over the work there, continuing a tradition of serving people with leprosy that had started as far back as 1895. And not only leprosy patients went to him for help.

'People suffering from all sorts of diseases come to Graham,' someone wrote, after visiting them. 'When I was there, they even had people calling at their home looking for treatment for snake bites!'

'What exactly do you do?' the Staines were often asked in letters from people who had never visited the work.

That was a hard question to answer as Graham was so multi-skilled that he did more or less anything that needed doing, from organising the Home, keeping the account books in order, helping patients in their rehabilitation, and teaching them how to make sabai grass products and handwoven goods for sale. He also preached and did outreach Christian work. Whenever he was able, Graham attended baptisms and Christian marriages, as he thought it was important to make a stand with local Christians. And in his 'spare time' he was involved in helping to translate the Bible into the local languages he knew so well. Gladys was very busy too, for as well as helping in the Home she had three children to look after. Esther was born in 1985, Philip in 1988 and Harold in 1992. The Staines were a happy, busy family, who loved where they lived and the work they did.

It was on 22nd January, 1999 that everything changed. Graham and his sons set out for Manoharpur to attend a jungle camp. Jungle camps were annual missionary events.

'They are so excited,' Gladys thought, as she waved goodbye to them. 'The boys just love having time on their own with their dad.'

After a long and exhausting day, Graham parked their station wagon, and then Philip and Harold cuddled down to sleep in the back. To protect them from the icy-cold, night wind, their dad hoisted a straw pad over the roof of the station wagon then settled down to sleep himself. Just after midnight, a group of men armed with sticks, axes and tridents, gathered round the station wagon. Screaming as they circled the vehicle, they hit out at it. The tyres were slashed. The windows were broken. What did they see as they looked inside? Was it the sight of a father praying with his two sons that so enraged them? Whatever it was, the results were terrible. Graham, Philip and Harold were attacked and stabbed with tridents. Straw was pushed under the station wagon, right under the petrol tank, and torched. In seconds the icy wind fanned the flames into an inferno from which there was no possible escape. The attackers watched the fire blaze and chased those who came to help put it out.

'Don't come near, or we'll kill you too,' the death-crazed men screamed to those who lived nearby.

One of Graham's friends, who was visiting Manoharpur, was within shouting distance. He heard the noise and made to race to find out what was wrong, not knowing the Staines were under attack. Grabbing the door handle, he discovered that the key had been turned on the outside. He didn't know what was happening, but he did know he could do nothing to help, whatever it was. By the time the man was freed, the terrible deed was done. All that was left was the charred remains of the station wagon and of Graham and his sons, who loved the Indian people enough to spend their lives serving them.

* * *

'My husband and our children have sacrificed their lives for this nation,' Gladys said later. 'But India is my home. I am happy to be here.'

And Esther, who had lost her father and both her young brothers, said, 'I praise God that he found my father worthy to die for Christ.'

Graham, Philip and Harold died for the sake of Jesus, and for the people of India, and Gladys and Esther remained to serve God and the people of that land. They will meet again one day, and when they do, there will be no more tears or pain, for these things have no place in heaven.

FACT FILE

Leprosy: We read a lot about leprosy in the Bible, and, in the gospels, we find stories about Jesus curing lepers. Now the disease is rarely known in the developed world and, if caught early, can be cured by medicine. However, it is still widespread in India and some other warm and poor countries. The disease tends to affect the extremities of the body. Because it kills the nerves, that means that people with leprosy cannot feel pain. This causes them real problems because they can seriously burn or cut themselves without knowing it.

Keynote: We often look for gratitude or even some reward from those we help. It is tempting to think that Graham did not get much reward for his services to the Indian people, since he and his sons were murdered there. But even if he had no reward on earth, he knew that he was pleasing his Father in heaven, and that he had a reward there which no one could take away from him.

Think: Even at the end of a happy Christmas day in Australia, Graham was thinking about the poor boy in India with leprosy, that he had seen in a photograph. He did not allow his comfort to blind him to the pain and suffering of others. This made Graham pray for these people and look to see how he could help them. Can you think of people anywhere in the world that you would like to help?

 Prayer: Lord Jesus, thank you for the cures for leprosy that are now available. But thank you even more for coming so that we can be cleansed from our sins. Please be with those who are suffering just now and comfort them. Amen.

Quiz

How much can you remember about the ten boys who didn't give in? Try answering these questions to find out.

Polycarp

1. What was used to tie the slaves together in the story that Polycarp's mother told him?

2. What did Polycarp see in his dream?

3. Which person from the Bible is Polycarp said to have met?

Alban

4. Where did the young Alban want to go to watch the chariot races?

5. What did people call London before it was known by that name?

6. Who was the emperor who gave the order to persecute Christians in Britain as well as Rome?

Sir John Oldcastle

7. Which country did John fight in to win his knighthood?

8. What was the name of the group that called him 'Good Lord Cobham'?

9. Where did the government lock John up?

Thomas Cranmer

10. What job did Thomas get as head of the Protestant church in England?

11. Who succeeded to the throne after Henry VIII?

12. Which hand did Thomas put into the fire first?

George Wishart

13. What were the bits of paper called that the Roman Church used to sell?

14. Where was the Scottish school that George taught in?

15. Where was George executed?

James Chalmers

16. Which country did James hear about when he was a teenager?

17. What did the painted men demand of James and his wife when they first arrived in New Guinea?

18. Who went with James to Goaribari Island?

Dietrich Bonhoeffer

19. What was across the road from the first house that Dietrich lived in?

20. Who became Reich Chancellor in 1932?

21. Which anti-Nazi church was Dietrich part of?

Nate Saint

22. What did Nate learn to assemble with his eyes closed while in the Air Cadet Training Program?

23. What day did Nate get married on?

24. How did Nate give presents to the Auca people?

Ivan Moiseyev

25. Where did the baby sleep in Vanya's house?

26. Where did Vanya's friends warn that he would be sent if he did not stop talking about God?

27. What did Vanya have to wear when he was made to stand outside in the cold all night?

Graham Staines

28. Which Australian state was Graham's book about?

29. What did Graham have for his Christmas dinner?

30. How did Graham learn the native languages in India?

How well did you do?

Turn over to find out ...

Quiz Answers

1. A rope

2. Himself being burned at the stake

3. The Apostle John

4. The Circus Maximus

5. Londinium

6. Septimus Severus

7. France

8. The Lollards

9. The Tower of London

10. Archbishop of Canterbury

11. Edward VI

12. His right hand

13. Indulgences

14. Montrose

15. St Andrews

16. Fiji

17. Knives, tomahawks and other weapons

18. Oliver Tomkins

19. A cemetery

20. Adolf Hitler

21. The Confessing Church

22. A Tommy gun

23. Valentine's Day

24. In a bucket suspended from the plane

25. On the shelf beside the stove

26. Siberia

27. His summer uniform

28. Queensland

29. A barbecue

30. By spending time with people who spoke to them.

Start collecting this series now!

Ten Boys who used their Talents:
ISBN 978-1-84550-146-4
Paul Brand, Ghillean Prance, C.S.Lewis,
C.T. Studd, Wilfred Grenfell, J.S. Bach,
James Clerk Maxwell, Samuel Morse,
George Washington Carver, John Bunyan.

Ten Girls who used their Talents:
ISBN 978-1-84550-147-1
Helen Roseveare, Maureen McKenna,
Anne Lawson, Harriet Beecher Stowe,
Sarah Edwards, Selina Countess of Huntingdon,
Mildred Cable, Katie Ann MacKinnon,
Patricia St. John, Mary Verghese.

Ten Boys who Changed the World:
ISBN 978-1-85792-579-1
David Livingstone, Billy Graham, Brother Andrew,
John Newton, William Carey, George Müller,
Nicky Cruz, Eric Liddell, Luis Palau,
Adoniram Judson.

Ten Girls who Changed the World:
ISBN 978-1-85792-649-1
Corrie Ten Boom, Mary Slessor,
Joni Eareckson Tada, Isobel Kuhn,
Amy Carmichael, Elizabeth Fry, Evelyn Brand,
Gladys Aylward, Catherine Booth, Jackie Pullinger.

Ten Boys who Made a Difference:
ISBN 978-1-85792-775-7
Augustine of Hippo, Jan Hus, Martin Luther,
Ulrich Zwingli, William Tyndale, Hugh Latimer,
John Calvin, John Knox, Lord Shaftesbury,
Thomas Chalmers.

Ten Girls who Made a Difference:
ISBN 978-1-85792-776-4
Monica of Thagaste, Catherine Luther,
Susanna Wesley, Ann Judson, Maria Taylor,
Susannah Spurgeon, Bethan Lloyd-Jones,
Edith Schaeffer, Sabina Wurmbrand,
Ruth Bell Graham.

Ten Boys who Made History:
ISBN 978-1-85792-836-5
Charles Spurgeon, Jonathan Edwards,
Samuel Rutherford, D L Moody,
Martin Lloyd Jones, A W Tozer, John Owen,
Robert Murray McCheyne, Billy Sunday,
George Whitfield.

Ten Girls who Made History:
ISBN 978-1-85792-837-2
Ida Scudder, Betty Green, Jeanette Li,
Mary Jane Kinnaird, Bessie Adams,
Emma Dryer, Lottie Moon, Florence Nightingale,
Henrietta Mears, Elisabeth Elliot.

Ten Boys who Didn't Give In:
ISBN 978-1-84550-035-1
Polycarp, Alban, Sir John Oldcastle
Thomas Cramer, George Wishart,
James Chalmers, Dietrich Bonhoeffer
Nate Saint, Ivan Moiseyev
Graham Staines.

Ten Girls who Didn't Give In:
ISBN 978-1-84550-036-8
Blandina, Perpetua, Lady Jane Grey,
Anne Askew, Lysken Dirks, Marion Harvey,
Margaret Wilson, Judith Weinberg,
Betty Stam, Esther John.

CHRISTIAN FOCUS PUBLICATIONS

Christian Focus | Christian Heritage | CF4K | Mentor

Christian Focus Publications publishes books for adults and children under its four main imprints: Christian Focus, CF4K, Mentor and Christian Heritage. Our books reflect our conviction that God's Word is reliable and Jesus is the way to know him, and live for ever with him.

Our children's publication list includes a Sunday School curriculum that covers pre-school to early teens, and puzzle and activity books. We also publish personal and family devotional titles, biographies and inspirational stories that children will love.

If you are looking for quality Bible teaching for children then we have an excellent range of Bible stories and age-specific theological books.

From pre-school board books to teenage apologetics, we have it covered!

Find us at our web page:
www.christianfocus.com

CF4 •K
Because you're never
too young to know Jesus